Doing Time

Writing Workshops in Prison

Carole Glasser Langille

Pottersfield Press, Lawrencetown Beach, Nova Scotia, Canada

Library and Archives Canada Cataloguing in Publication
Title: Doing time : writing workshops in prison / Carole Glasser Langille.
Names: Langille, Carole Glasser, author.
Identifiers: Canadiana (print) 20190119861 | Canadiana (ebook) 20190121173 | ISBN 9781988286921 (softcover) | ISBN 9781988286938 (EPUB)
Subjects: LCSH: Prisoners' writings. | LCSH: Writers' workshops. | LCSH: Prisoners—Services for. | LCSH: Criminals—Rehabilitation. | LCSH: Creative writing—Therapeutic use. | LCSH: Imprisonment— Psychological aspects.
Classification: LCC HV9281 .L36 2019 | DDC 365/.661—dc23

Cover design: Gail LeBlanc

Pottersfield Press gratefully acknowledges the financial support of the Government of Canada for our publishing activities. We also acknowledge the support of the Canada Council for the Arts and the Province of Nova Scotia which has assisted us to develop and promote our creative industries for the benefit of all Nova Scotians.

Pottersfield Press
248 Leslie Road
East Lawrencetown, Nova Scotia, Canada, B2Z 1T4
Website: www.PottersfieldPress.com
To order, phone 1-800-NIMBUS9 (1-800-646-2879) www.nimbus.ns.ca

Printed in Canada

Pottersfield Press is committed to protecting our natural environment. This book is made of material from well-managed FSC®-certified forests and other controlled sources.

"You must let suffering speak, if you want to hear the truth."

          – Cornel West

"For me, a storyteller, he's like … somebody who gets contraband across a frontier."

          – John Berger

I would like to begin by acknowledging that I wrote this manuscript on Mi'kma'ki, the ancestral and unceded territory of the Mi'kmaq, continued on the unceded territory of the Coast Salish People, then returned to Mi'kma'ki to complete the writing. I am deeply grateful.

To the men and women who were in my writing workshops at the correctional facility, and to the social work students who helped with these workshops, I dedicate this book. I wrote *Doing Time* to thank you for your trust and generosity in sharing your stories. And to honour you. And to thank the corrections officers for the work they do.

My first impulse was to ask everyone for permission to include your names and stories. But I could not get in touch with all of you and decided instead to change names and disguise details so no one I write about would be identified. I have also amalgamated some workshops to avoid repetition. Everything I have written happened, though I write from my observations and perspective alone.

One inmate said to me, "Tell our stories, be our advocate" and I decided I would. Without you there would be no stories to tell.

Contents

PROLOGUE

When I read Mark Salzman's *True Notebooks: A Writer's Year at Juvenile Hall* in 2004[1], a book about teaching writing to young inmates, many who committed murder, I thought, *Yes, this is exactly what I want to do.* But at the time I lived in Lunenburg, on Nova Scotia's South Shore, and the nearest prison was over an hour and a half away. I was not confident or comfortable about driving that distance, especially in winter.

I told my friend Eleanor Williams that I wanted to give workshops in prison. Eleanor was eighty-five then. Five years earlier, on her eightieth birthday, she said to me, Eighty isn't old, you know. Eleanor had four children and many grandchildren and still had time for me. She treated me like family. Of all my friends, Eleanor was the one who would be sure to ask how my car was holding up. She'd read poems I'd written and question certain lines. We talked about stories that were published in *The New Yorker* and novels we hated or loved.

She suggested I contact her granddaughter Maya about volunteering. Maya didn't work at a prison, but at a drop-in centre whose goal was to empower young people living with mental illness. I did meet with Maya and did give writing workshops at the centre where she worked.

It wasn't until 2014 that I began giving work-shops at the Central Nova Scotia Correctional Facility. The roulette wheel of destiny often takes a while to align with desire. The older I get the more I see that timing often works in our favour, that waiting can be advantageous.

I valued Eleanor's insights. Once I asked if she felt closer to her children or grandchildren and she said, I don't like to compare love. She was just a few years younger than my mother would have been, but she was never a mother to me. She was always a friend. My sons loved her too.

I didn't know why I wanted to work with prisoners so much but I thought, Perhaps working in the prison will help me find out. As Bryan Stevenson says in his book *Just Mercy: A Story of Justice and Redemption*, "We are all broken by something. We have all hurt some-one and have been hurt. ... There is a strength, a power even, in understanding brokenness, because embracing our brokenness creates a need and desire for mercy, and perhaps a corresponding need to show mercy."[2]

It is a subject I would have liked to discuss with Eleanor. She saw things that weren't immediately ob-vious. I would have liked to talk with her about timing as well.

But Eleanor died in 2011. She was ninety-three. I see now that ninety-three isn't old. In whatever time I have left, I hope to be helpful to those who might find my assistance and encouragement valuable.

CHAPTER ONE

A few years after I moved to a rural community near Hubbards, about sixty kilometres from Lunenburg and about forty-five minutes from the Central Nova Scotia Correctional Facility, I wrote to the John Howard Society, outlining a writing workshop I proposed to give. I had an interview with the director of the society in the beginning of 2014 and he arranged a meeting with a committee in charge of programming at the prison. The director came to the meeting as well.

I explained how I planned to give the workshops and why I wanted to give them. Creativity is a life force, I said. I wanted to inspire inmates to write about what mattered to them. Writing clarifies thoughts, I said, and when thinking is clearer, actions become more comprehensible.

Every creative act is empowering, generating energy and self-worth. The role of a poet is "to help people live their lives," Wallace Stevens said. This is why I read poetry. This is why I wanted to bring poems to inmates. Because poetry makes visible what cannot be seen. Because poetry takes familiar, everyday occurrences and reveals them to be extraordinary. As M.S. Merwin says, "Poetry addresses individuals in their most intimate, private, frightened and elated moments

... because it comes closer than any other art form to addressing what cannot be said."[3]

But I did not say this to the committee in the prison. I had not been asked to give a lecture. Instead, I read poems I would hand out and explained exercises I would give. I hoped the poems would speak for themselves. I was in luck. The head of the programming committee was looking for new programs for inmates and I was given permission to volunteer.

After the presentation, a security-risk officer showed me around the prison. He said he saw all prisoners as bad and dangerous. Otherwise, why would they be here? he asked.

I listened. I didn't disagree. I wanted to give the workshops.

They are manipulative, he continued. They'll try to get you to do things for them. I know that people like you think prisoners are poor, misunderstood people, but I know better, and you'll see soon enough.

I was told that in March, after I would have already begun the workshops, I would have to go to the prison for a three-hour orientation given by this man. How would I sit through it? But I nodded. I thanked him.

I learned the word "remand" means waiting in jail for a trial, without being convicted of a crime. Later I found out that in Canadian jails, those on remand outnumber inmates who are sentenced. In 2014 there were approximately 13,650 adults held in remand, awaiting trial or sentencing, and 10,364 adults in sentenced-custody in the provinces and territories.[4]

Before I left, the security-risk officer talked to me about riots in the prison. He showed a display of weapons prisoners had made or that were smuggled into the prison, and noted the orifices of the body in which they were smuggled.

On the way home I stopped at a store and bought and ate an entire large chocolate bar, something I don't often do. I felt so worn down. Weeks after that, when I gave the workshops, I did not feel enervated as I did in that orientation meeting. Often I was sad when each session was over, but I left with a sense of hope and possibility.

Each week, when I walked down those windowless halls, the iron doors clanging behind me, I felt again and again that the pain and longing in that crowded building created a spiritual intensity that made this a holy place, a dwelling whose inhabitants must be appreciated and treated with care. I had the privilege of hearing many of their stories. I wanted to honour them for their trust.

CHAPTER TWO

THURSDAY, FEBRUARY 27, 2014

I am told I will be working with men on the North Wing. I've signed in, locked my coat and purse in the locker, put on the bullet-proof vest they've given me. As the guard leads me down one hall and up another, our stride punctuated by stopping and waiting to be buzzed through several locked doors, I try to memorize where I am going. I do not have a good sense of direction.

The workshop is held in a concrete room painted off-white. There are no windows, no other colour except the red fire extinguisher and the clock on the wall with its red numerals. The triangular desks are arranged in a semicircle. The chairs are heavy so prisoners cannot use them as weapons. At first I think they are filled with concrete, but later learn they are packed with sand.

Knowing the door will lock behind the guard, l ask, just before he leaves to get the participants, what happens in case of fire. He points out that the room is concrete; nothing can burn. The workshops too, I will soon understand, will be more a meeting place of tears than fire. And yet, as soon as the inmates come into the room, something ignites in me. I am very glad to be here.

Seven inmates wearing orange jumpsuits file in to the room when the guard opens the door. Each takes a seat in the semicircle. Hi, I'm Carole Langille, I say introducing myself. I tell them I am from New York City and feel very lucky that Nova Scotia is now my home. I tell them I teach in the Creative Writing Program at Dalhousie University. I am not a professor, I'm a lecturer and only teach one course, but I want them to know that I bring the same material to these workshops that I bring to my classes at the university.

I ask the men to introduce themselves as well and they each share their first name and where they are from. Marvin, a pale man with freckles, speaks very fast and I have to ask him to slow down so I can understand him. Jonah asks if I can come on Wednesdays instead of Thursdays so he will not have to miss gym and I tell him I can do that. He is a young compact man with a chiselled face and a short afro (when I describe this later to a friend of my son, I am told it is a short top with fade), and is so handsome he could be a model. There does not seem to be tension between the white, Indigenous, and Black men in the room.

I hand out the poem "How I Go to the Woods" by Mary Oliver.[5] The poem ends by saying if the poet has ever invited you to go into the woods with her, she must love you very much. For their first assignment, which is due next week, I ask them to write, in detail, a few paragraphs about a place that is or was special to them and to write about who took them to this place.

I also give out the poem "To My Room" by Robert Berold.[6] We talk about how a location can feel alive. In the poem, Berold addresses his room. He writes, *I've slept three thousand nights in your arms.* He ends the poem with the lines,

The trees are coming into leaf today.
I tell you this slowly because you've never been outside.

When the men leave to go back to their cells, I hear Marvin say to the guard, It's about time we had a good workshop! I especially like Marvin and Jonah, both enthusiastic about reading poems and writing.

WEDNESDAY, MARCH 5

Today is my second workshop in the prison. I wait at the front desk for the corrections officer or one of the guards to take me to the program room where the workshop will be held. Though I've been here before, I know I will not find the North Wing on my own.

There are six inmates in the workshop today. Marvin is not here. The others say he is in lockdown – he broke some rule. They have him hanging from the walls in chains, Kendrick says, and I gasp. They all laugh and I say, I am gullible – please don't tell me things that aren't true.

It doesn't yet click that lockdown is solitary confinement. An inmate is placed behind a metal door and has no contact with anyone except for an occasional guard. I wonder how long prisoners are put in solitary. Kendrick may have joked that the punishment is medieval, but he has hit upon the right metaphor.

The men have brought in the assignment I gave at the first workshop – to write, in detail, about a place that was special to them. All six have written about being near water – the lake, the ocean, a river that brought them comfort. Jonah said the poem by Mary Oliver made him smile and reminded him of his favourite place, a lake near his house where he used to walk his dogs. In his essay he writes: I know the lake, and the lake knows me. He is very attentive and respectful when he talks to the other participants and to me.

Eric, a man in his twenties with light brown hair and no tattoos on his arms, which is surprising in this place, asks me what *my* favourite place is. I tell him I love going off the path when I walk in the woods. I am afraid a bear will be there or some crazed animal will dart out at me, though I know that is very unlikely. I say, My husband is not an alarmist and he explains there are no bears in the woods behind our house, but still, I worry.

Jonah says, My aunt is an – what did you say – alarmist. Someone walks past our house and she looks out the window and worries about who is passing by.

Ella, a student working in the prison, is the only non-prisoner with me in the workshop. She is a young woman studying for her social work degree. She says she will type up what the men write, deciphering their script and correcting misspellings, so that, after a month, we can have all the men's pieces typed and photocopied and each man can have a booklet of the group's work.

This does not happen. Ella is so helpful, but also very busy. When she walks me to the main desk she says, The guys are really open here. They don't have to put on an act.

At the end of the workshop I pass a guard in the hall. He says, I can't believe these guys like poetry.

The inmates are still in the hall, but when they are no longer there I say, They are interested in writing and sharing what they are thinking and feeling. I don't ask them to write poems. I bring in poems that explore various topics. We discuss the theme of the poem and then I ask them to write a few paragraphs about their own experiences that relate to our discussion.

One corrections officer says, It's probably better that I don't come into the workshop, because I would not believe these guys are sincere. I'd inhibit them. It is honest of her to say this.

Something I remember vividly about the workshops on the North Wing happens when the men are going back to their cells. As they are filing out I shake their hands and thank them for participating. Thank you, they say, thank you for coming here.

It takes a while to discover that the stories I hear in these workshops are a fire that focuses light on what is not easily seen. Their stories will linger in me, as burning embers.

WEDNESDAY, MARCH 12

We talk about metaphor and simile. *She stood on her own dark shadow as if it were a bridge she was afraid to cross* is a line from Jason Heroux's poem "Flower Shop" that I give out.[7] We talk about why comparing one image to another dramatizes both images and makes each more visual. I talk about how many metaphorical bridges in this life we're all afraid to cross.

Then I give out the poem "My Father's Love Letters" by Yusef Komunyakaa.[8] The men understand details I did not comprehend when I first read the poem. I ask what the following lines mean:

> *The gleam of a five-pound wedge*
> *On the concrete floor*
> *Pulled a sunset*
> *Through the doorway of his toolshed ...*

Antonio says, The wood is wedged in the door, leaving it open, and the people in the toolshed can see the sun set through this space.

It's the verb that makes that line come alive, I say. *Pulled* in the sunset! When you write your stories think carefully about verbs, I tell the men.

Edward spends his time drawing instead of writing. He explains that he does not know how to read but "My Father's Love Letters" inspired him, since the man in that poem couldn't read either, but was still smart. Eric, Jonah, Antonio, and Kendrick all admire Ed's drawings of people, houses, animals, buildings. They are beautiful, I agree.

I explain that the poem works because it is so specific and detailed:

> *We sat in the quiet brutality*
> *Of voltage meters & pipe threaders,*
> *Lost between sentences ...*

Why brutality of voltage meters and pipe threaders? I ask. Jonah says maybe the conversation between father and son has some brutality in it. The voltage meters are metal, he says, and metal can be sharp and jagged and so, sort of brutal.

The poem ends,

> *This man*
> *Who stole roses & hyacinth*
> *For his yard, would stand there*

With eyes closed & fists balled,
Laboring over a simple word, almost
Redeemed by what he tried to say.

Kendrick asks what hyacinths look like. I try to describe a hyacinth. I say it's a bulb, like a tulip, but its blossom has lots of little flowers growing together. This is not a good description. I tell them I will bring in a photo.

I ask how they feel about writing about someone who did something wrong. It can be a fictional character.

I did something wrong. That's why I'm here, Eric says. I did plenty wrong.

I ask if he wants to write about it for the homework assignment and he says, Okay. The other men say they will write too.

Jonah says, Tell me what metaphor is again? When I explain, he asks for an example and I say, *Chaos is a friend of mine* and he writes it down. Bob Dylan said that, I add, and ask the men if they know who Bob Dylan is. No one does.

Ella, the young social work student, explains, He's the one who wrote "Blowing in the Wind" but they are not familiar with that song. I mention "It Ain't Me, Babe" and "All Along the Watch Tower" and "You Have To Serve Somebody," but no one knows these songs. I ask if they've heard "Knocking on Heaven's Door," a Dylan song also written decades before they were born, and Eric says he thinks he heard Guns N' Roses sing it.

But the next week Eric is not in class, and the others have not done the assignment. I too have been neglectful and forgotten to bring in a photo of a hyacinth.

I decide to ask them to write in class, as well as bring in an assignment, and this plan works best. The in-class assignment for the following week is to write about a memory they have of something that happened with a friend or sibling when they were younger. I say, If the memory lingers, even if the incident seems trivial, it is important to you in some way.

Jonah writes about an event that happened in fourth grade. I tell him I want more details. So the next week he brings in the piece after he adds wonderful descriptions and interesting information.

He describes his excitement in grade five when he won gold in a boxing tournament. Afterwards, at lunch hour, he and his two best friends split up and went their separate ways home. He recounts in detail the spot where he was hit by a truck and why he did not tell his mother when he got home late for lunch, though she knew something was wrong.

When he limped back to school, the principal called his name over the loudspeaker. His heart started racing as if he were being hit all over again. It turned out the man in the truck was in the principal's office. He explained that he'd gone into the building to call the ambulance and wanted to know why Jonah had left. For some reason Jonah had felt in the wrong. He ends the piece by saying that repercussions from the accident remain to this day. Everyone in the group loves the piece.

Ella is no longer here but Kaiya, another social work student, is a great help during the workshop. She tells me she is tutoring Edward to read. She says, He knows how to read, but he is dyslexic and needs help.

After I have been giving the workshop for a few weeks, Eric asks, Why do you come here? Do you volunteer?

I thank him for the question. Yes, I volunteer, I tell him. I say, I love poetry and want to share it. I tell him that all week I look forward to coming to the workshop.

I am so glad, at this moment, that I do not get paid to give these workshops.

Oh, you're a good person, Eric says.

How could I not want to be here?

WEDNESDAY, MARCH 19

I hand out the poem by Campbell McGrath entitled "Two Songs" and we discuss the first stanza, "North Carolina":[9]

The more you allow the figures of black, silent trees
glimpsed by night from the window of a train near
Fayetteville into your heart, the greater the burden you
must carry with you on your journey, and the sooner
you will come to question your ability to endure it,
and the stronger your conviction to sing.

I ask the men what they think the black silent trees represent and why must we let them into our hearts. Once we do this, why is the burden great, and why is our conviction to sing even stronger?

Kendrick says, The black silent trees, that's the blues. Once you feel something, you can't unfeel it.

The blues, which originated in the Southern United States by African Americans, is certainly a conviction to sing in the face of great burdens. Kendrick has made such a powerful analogy.

We talk about vulnerability and how, paradoxically, being open and vulnerable can make us stronger. I quote Lao Tzu: *Nothing is softer than water but it wears away rock. To compel the unyielding, it has no equal.*

I give them the following quote by Philo of Alexandria: *Be kind, for everyone you know is fighting a great battle.*

Sometimes we think people are out to get us, but their actions have little to do with us. If we recognized how much pain they were in, we would sympathize with them, I say. I ask the inmates to write a few paragraphs about someone they interacted with which illustrates this point.

Antonio's piece is about being hospitalized, when he was in first or second grade, to correct a problem with his hip. He had to use crutches and wear shoes with a very thick heel. It seems, from his description, that he was pigeon-toed. His mother rarely came to visit and he was alone day after day. The nurses were nice to him and gave him oatmeal cookies and ginger ale and he looked forward to being with them each day. I ask why his mother didn't visit and he says she had to look after his brothers and sisters. After he got out of the hospital he was still on crutches. He felt like a freak. But the operation didn't take so he had to go back for another operation, or, as he says, more torture.

When he got older he was very angry at his mother and started acting out. Finally she took him to the Juvenile Detention Centre and told the corrections officer that she couldn't take care of him any longer and left him there. He watched her walk away. She didn't even turn around, he said. He was thirteen and he didn't see her again for another four years.

I say, That is so sad that you were alone in the hospital. That is a great trauma in your life. And sad you were taken to the authorities at such a young age.

Antonio says, Now you are making me feel like I am going to cry, and he does start crying though he tries to hide it, brushing his eyes with the heel of his palm. I say, No tears in the writer, no tears in the reader, but I am close to crying too. I say that only when we have the courage to be honest does the reader get something from the writing.

Antonio ends his piece saying he was angry at his mother but he knows she had burdens too. She was sent to residential school where she was beaten and had to eat her own vomit, and was touched inappropriately and wasn't allowed to speak the Mi'kmaw language. I tell Antonio what a great piece he's written.

At this time there is some wonderful synchronicity. A student at Dalhousie University starts a literary magazine. When she hears I am giving workshops in the prison, she asks if I can invite prisoners to submit work. They have no emails or access to computers, but I tell the men about the journal, and ask if I can type up their work and submit it. I tell them there is no guarantee their work will be published, that it is not easy to get something published. They all say I can submit their work.

I type up several pieces and send them to the student who publishes the journal.

WEDNESDAY, MARCH 26

Marvin is in lockdown again. The corrections officer, a young woman, tells me he often acts out, though she knows he is interested in the workshop. Nolan, who looked at me with such kindness and interest during the last session, did not come to the workshop. The other inmates tell me he is in court today.

Kendrick has written about his brother who was murdered and how angry he was at the man who killed him. But there were things this man did not know – for example, that he was related, distantly, to the family. This man is in jail now, and Kendrick prays to let go of his anger. Though he hasn't completely let go, he feels a big burden has been lifted from him, because he is not as angry.

Eric writes about a friend who was unfaithful to his girlfriend and ended up giving her chlamydia. He gives reasons why he thinks his friend was unfaithful. It is an interesting story full of details.

Jonah told how he would always give money to friends when they needed it, or give them a lift, but then he felt like people were just using him. Now he has fewer friends but truer friends. His mother told him, Don't be giving things away to people who don't care.

When I respond positively to the piece, I mistakenly say Noah instead of Jonah. Jonah is not happy about my mistake. I apologize. He wants to know why I've called him Noah. He says kids in school used to make fun of him by calling him Noah. One of the men in the workshop says, Hey, she's human. And she apologized.

Afterwards Marlis, the corrections officer, tells me that Jonah is in prison because he and an accomplice are accused of murdering a man they lured to a location. It is rumoured Jonah and the accomplice had dealings with him in the past. I don't know how accurate these details are. She says he is very secretive and doesn't talk much about this.

The crime is hard to believe. Jonah is so dignified, intelligent, kind to the other men. He is profoundly interested in learning and responds deeply to poems. I know little about his life, the friends who influenced him, the code among men his age, and what it means to be a man in a world where the options are limited.

I say to a neighbour, If we grew up with their experiences and their influences, we would act as these inmates act. She disagrees. I don't argue with her, but I wonder, does she think people are born with different amounts of morality? Of course, not everyone who grows up in the same environment, good or bad, reacts in the same way to the same situations. But why are some people ravaged by hardship? And if they are, why would we, having their experience, be any different?

Bessel van der Kolk says one of the most devastating effects of trauma is that it often damages a sense of purpose and derails one of the most important tools people have to help them live, the urge to prepare for the future. Trauma can make people feel there is nothing they can do to prevent the inevitable and this can lead to "'learned helplessness,' a phenomenon that is critical for understanding and treating traumatized and humiliated human beings."[10]

Before I worked in the prison, I had never been in one room with so many people suffering from trauma.

WEDNESDAY, APRIL 2

I had to miss the previous workshop because of a snowstorm. Today there are only four men here: Jonah, Edward, Antonio, and Kendrick. They've written about something that happened with a friend or brother or sister. In order to inspire them, I'd given out "The Trick" by Julie Bruck at the last workshop.[11] "The Trick" is a poem about childhood memories. In the poem three or four boys

> *grab our hats and run*
> *with impossible suddenness, schoolbags slung*
> *like ammo belts across their eight-year-old chests.*
> *We jammed the hats our mothers bought*
> *deep in our pockets like charms – anything*
> *to deflect their rough attentions,*
> *though I knew it meant they liked us:*
> *I had two brothers and understood*
> *to love meant to torment.*

We'd talked about why the little girls in the poem appeared to be

> *small monks who remained,*
> *to all appearances, untouched.*

Isn't that a great metaphor, I'd said.

Kendrick said, Yes, we pretend we're one thing, but really we're another. He said, We think it's safer to hide what's happening.

When I gave out the assignment, Jonah asked if he had to write about a sad experience and I say, No, I'd love to hear about a happy time.

Eric said he did not have any good memories. But by the end of the workshop he said he'd thought of something to write.

Today, Jonah reads his story first. He tells how he used to work with his friend when they were both sixteen. His friend, who helped support his mother and sister, worked double shifts cleaning stores. Jonah would drive him to the job where they both worked, but the friend had to take two buses to get to the second job and he would tell Jonah how hard it was to get there. One day, when the friend was cleaning a Tim Hortons store, he found a cup that did not have the rim rolled down. He rolled it down and it turned out it was the winning cup. He won a car. Jonah was very happy for his friend.

What a great story, we all agree.

Edward tells a story about a car as well, but this new car, which his older brother had just gotten, was not what it seemed. An undercover cop had befriended his brother and this man arrested Edward's brother because of how the car was obtained. Edward did not go into the specifics. He did say he thought the cop tricked him, an eight-year-old boy, into saying something he should not have said and that might have been used in court to implicate his brother. Did Edward think he was responsible in any way?

Kendrick writes about how when he was little he thought all dogs were trained to fight with each other, that's what people did with their dogs in the neighbourhood, and he got his dogs fighting – a beautiful St. Bernard and a German shepherd. When his father came home and found out, he beat him. Kendrick never let his dogs fight again.

Antonio tells how, when he was eight, his family moved to Italy, where his father was from, and how beautiful it was on the farm. He used to sit under the plum tree and eat plums. The turkeys would chase him and he was glad when they were finally slaughtered. After a few years they all moved to Toronto and then the family split up. But in Italy his family was still a family.

Kaiya says the guys were not pleased when she had not written something for the last session, so she was determined to write something this time and she reads her piece. I hadn't brought in anything I'd written, but I recited a poem I'd memorized from one of my books that begins, *This is where we come to find our parents*. When I finish, Kendrick says, That was beautiful and Antonio says, Yes it was. Jonah says, That was great. Edward says, I like the way you read, and I like the expressions you make and I like the poems you bring in.

Thanks so much, I say, and Jonah says again, Yeah, that was beautiful.

I say, Aren't you nice, and he smiles. Then he asks if they are going to get a certificate when the course ends, so Kaiya offers to print up certificates.

As I am leaving, Jonah says, You know it's a good workshop when it lasts an hour longer than the schedule says.

THURSDAY, APRIL 17

In April I am away for a week in New York, visiting family. When I go back to the prison, three men from past workshops are there – Jonah, Antonio, Edward – and two new participants, Nick and Jake. Kaiya is not there and I am the only non-prisoner in the room. In fact, the guards ask me if I can go to the room on my own, but I don't think I can find my way, so one guard accompanies me. Marlis isn't staying for the workshop so she leaves the intercom with me. When she sees Jonah she says, So Joey, you write poems!

He says, My name is Jonah, not Joey. Close in age, they look like popular and attractive young people in a college classroom. In another life, assuming they are both straight, they might have been dating each other. Except here, Marlis has all the power. Though she does not mean to make Jonah uncomfortable, I can feel him bristle at the insult of being called by a nickname.

I hand out the poem "What I Hated," by the South African poet Robert Berold,[12] which begins,

> *What I hated*
> *was the way they used to laugh*
> *the way pain and confusion*
> *was funny to them.*

We talk about South Africa and what the word kaffir means – an offensive term referring to Black people in apartheid South Africa. I ask the men if they were ever offended by something, yet felt they had to accept what they found upsetting, in order to "belong." Then I ask them to write a piece during the week entitled either "What I Hated" or "What I Loved."

Nick, the new participant, says he has written a great poem but doesn't remember it. I nod and say I look forward to hearing his work. His words seemed a metaphor for how we all want to contribute but often believe we have nothing to share.

I hand out a poem by Thich Nhat Hanh, "Call Me by My True Names."[13] In the poem are these two verses:

> *I am the child in Uganda, all skin and bones,*
> *my legs as thin as bamboo sticks,*
> *and I am the arms merchant, selling deadly*
> > *weapons to Uganda.*
> *I am the twelve-year-old girl, refugee on a small*
> > *boat,*

who throws herself into the ocean after being
raped by a sea pirate,
and I am the pirate, my heart not yet capable of
seeing and loving.

Nick starts laughing. I say, These guys have already been here for four sessions so they know this is serious, but this is your first session and I see you don't yet know how things work.

He says, No, I was just surprised that you are so passionate. You don't see many people who are so passionate. It's good you like poetry so much.

I'm embarrassed that I reprimanded him. Sorry I overreacted, I say.

Jonah reads his piece about the relationship between him and his girlfriend. He says this was his first relationship, but her third, and she had been hurt so was not as trusting. Jonah was friends with her father, and her father told him to stand by his daughter, because she didn't always act right. Jonah, who was living with his girlfriend, says that sometimes she would leave, or sometimes he would leave and go back to his parents.

I tell him how much I like what he has written and ask him if he can give more details. Let us know why you left, what happened, what you said and what she said, and what enabled you to forgive and trust her. I ask him to describe what she looks like and how he and his girlfriend met. I say, Write as if you are taking a camera and filming what happened, so readers feel as if they are there.

Nick asks for a pencil and I say, This is the time to listen to Jonah finish his piece and Nick says, I just wanted to write down what you said.

Oh, now my ego is flattered, I say, and give him a pencil. I apologize for being bossy.

Jonah ends his piece saying how hard it was for him when they fought because he cared for her so much. I tell Jonah that I appreciate his piece and how tender it is. I say I hope he will continue writing about the relationship as I'd like to hear more of his insights.

When it is time to go the door is locked, as usual, and the men tell me what to do. Press the buzzer, they explain, and say: Five guys going back to North 4 from program.

THURSDAY, APRIL 24

I drive to the prison and when I walk in the front door I am told there is a lockdown. Guards are searching the West Wing, and there are not enough guards available to open the North Wing. Marlis asks if I want to go home. No, I say, I'll wait. The guards let me walk to North Wing on my own. I wait in Marlis's office for forty minutes and finally I am able to give the workshop.

Jonah, Edward, Antonio, Jake, and Nick are here as well as a new guy, Gabe. Kaiya is here as well.

Jonah says he was disappointed when he thought there wouldn't be a workshop. Antonio reads his piece first – about what he loves. He writes about the sweat lodge. They give a sweat lodge every two weeks at the prison. All my relations, he says respectfully when he enters the sweat. He writes how he feels humble and renewed after the sweat. It is so hot there, he wants to ask them to open the door flap of the tent but he waits until someone else asks. He leans close to the floor to get a few breaths of cool air.

Then Jonah reads a poem about what he hates: being chosen last. He says, A poem is usually short, right? Jake says he is not ready to read his, could he go last. He says he might not read the entire piece. He wasn't even going to come but Jonah told him, You wrote the piece, so why not come.

Thank you, Jonah, for encouraging him, I say.

I tell them I feel privileged to hear their pieces; we're all privileged to hear them, and it is generous of them to share what they write. Everyone learns something from these stories, I say. But if it's not the right time for you to share, that's fine too.

Nick reads his next. He says it isn't his story, it is fiction, though it is in the first person. In it the character says he hated that he couldn't get bail, that he was locked up, that the judge smelled bad, that his woman was giving up on him. Then he hanged himself. Nick explained that this was about the guy in the cell next to him. He saw the guy was feeling down and wanted to talk to him, but didn't. Later he heard the guy kick the chair out from under him. He felt bad he never talked to the guy before he killed himself.

That must have been such a trauma for you, Nick, Kaiya says. I ask him to give advice to the person in the story. What would the narrator tell him, to give him hope, if the man were still alive? Nick says he doesn't know. I ask if we can go around the room and if people can give suggestions. I ask if it is possible, in some way, to be free, even when you are in prison.

Antonio says, I'd tell him everything passes. Jonah says, I'd ask, How can I help you? These are both powerful things to say, I tell them.

Gabe, who has not come to the workshop before,

says, I am amazed how everybody has so much to say and is so personal.

Jake reads his next. He tells how he hated being an army brat, going from base to base. Just when he made friends in Halifax, his family moved to Seattle, Washington, and just when he made friends there his family moved again. In high school he got in with the wrong crowd. His family moved back to Seattle and he had a girlfriend – a beautiful girl with long blonde hair and blue eyes. She believed in him. He became a better person because of her. Then one evening they were at a party and he was drinking too much and they got into a fight. She called a friend to pick her up, but he was drunk too. The friend had an accident on the way home and she died. Jake's voice trembles as he reads his piece. I can feel his depth of grief. The story impacts all of us.

Gabe says, I knew you guys but didn't know you could write like this. I don't know what to say. I don't think I should even be here. I wish I had been here since the beginning.

It is my last session with this group and I tell them I will miss them and that I enjoyed working with them so much. I say I want to ask them something. Can they protect themselves and their talent, and not give way to petty anger, and keep writing and telling their stories? I want to say so much more. They deserve so much more. It's painful to me that I will probably never see these men again.

After the workshop Kaiya says she has never seen the guys so calm.

CHAPTER THREE

When I hear back from the editor who started the literary journal and who was reading the work from the men on North Wing, the six weeks are over and I am working in another part of the prison. But she has good news to tell me. She has accepted Antonio's story. She asks if I can get his biography. I no longer have contact with Antonio but I get in touch with Kaiya, the social work student who still works on the North Wing. I ask if she can let Antonio know his story was accepted, and if he can read the typed version I submitted. I ask if she can get a biography from him as well. This is the email I get back from her:

> Dear Carole and the Editor of The Literary Magazine,
> Antonio has gone over the changes and is fine with them. He has said he would like the piece to be called 'Mother and Son.'
> This is the bio he wrote:
> Antonio was born in Toronto, Ontario, to an Italian father and native Mi'kmaq mother. Because of his dual heritage he refers to himself as 'wopajo.' He is the fourth of five children. After his father's death, he and his mother left

Toronto in the 1990s to return to
her Mi'kmaq reservation. He is
presently incarcerated at the Central
Nova Scotia Correctional Facility in
Dartmouth, Nova Scotia. He says he
enjoys writing because he can write
things that hurt too much to say
aloud.
      Antonio says you can use any or
all of this.
      Thank you both again for doing
this. Antonio was incredibly proud
and very pleased, as are many of the
staff. It has been a delightful day
in the facility because of this great
news!

Wop, I know, is a derogatory term for Italian. Only later do I learn that Arapaho are First Nations people.

I am so happy for Antonio. I want him to feel honoured. His courage to explore his history, and the care he took to record it, deserves honour. But Jonah's piece is also powerful and the literary magazine was only able to accept one piece. If Jonah were in university he'd excel; he is passionate about learning. But here, there are few ways for inmates to be admired.

I'd typed up Jonah's piece as well and sent it to the newsletter put out by a local prisoner-advocate group. They agree to print it. I am so glad that now Jonah too has had a piece accepted for publication.

The newsletter comes out months after they'd accepted the piece, but once it is finally printed, I am able to send several copies to the prison, which the corrections officer gives Jonah. In his bio Jonah wrote:

```
I am a family man and enjoy
spending time with my kids and
having play dates. I am also a
graduate of the class of ___ in
which I received an award for
valedictorian of my course.
```

I did not know Jonah had children or had been a valedictorian. When you've committed a crime, everything else is rendered insignificant. How many gifts and accomplishments that these young men achieved remain unknown?

From Dr. Angela Davis's inaugural Viola Desmond Legacy Lecture, October 16, 2018[14]

People ... are in prison whether they committed reprehensible harms against other human beings, whether they committed minor acts against property, whether they are behind bars because they never had significant opportunities to learn, to receive mental health care, to live in decent housing, etcetera. People who are in prison have been designated as those who are divested of basic civil rights. They have been deprived of civil life and thus effectively relegated to a place of civil death. ...

It is behind jail and prison walls that we discover the worst modes of violence, officially condoned state violence, violence linked to the disciplinary process, gender violence promoted by the institution against men, against women, against trans and gender non-conforming prisoners, violence against the body, violence against the mind, violence against the spirit. This violence is never entirely contained by prison walls but rather exists in a symbiotic relation with violences in the larger society. It is not accidental that in jails and prisons all over the world there are disproportionate numbers of Black people, brown people, Indigenous people, people from the global south.

Prevention of deaths in custody[15]

Suicide is the leading cause of unnatural death in custody accounting for about one-in-five deaths in custody in any given year.

A disproportionate number of prison suicides occur in segregation units.

The number of prison deaths attributable to "natural" causes has increased (two-thirds of all deaths) reflecting an aging inmate population and chronic health conditions.

Safe custody indicators have slipped over the past decade[16]

Admissions to administrative segregation increased by 15.5%

Incidents of prison self-injury have tripled

Involuntary transfers increased by 46%

Inmate assaults have more than doubled

CHAPTER FOUR

THURSDAY, MAY 22

There are only three inmates who come to the first workshop I give on the women's wing – Macey, Rena, and Ruth. The social work student says that working with women will be more challenging than the men because many are addicts. The Central Nova Scotia Correctional Facility houses 322 men but only forty-eight women.

Ruth is in her late forties or early fifties, the other women, younger. Macey, her light brown skin clear, her dark brown eyes bright, is in her early twenties and very alive. Rena, skinny, her skin dry, her blue eyes dull, looks to be in her late thirties, but she may be younger. I wonder if she is sick.

The first day of the workshop, I hand out a page to each woman on which I've written a different line from a favourite poet. I ask the women to write a second line and then pass the page to the woman on her right, who will write a third line and pass the page on until it arrives back to the woman who was handed the page originally and who will read the finished poem aloud. At the end of the exercise there are six poems with

lines from all six people – three inmates, me, Hallie
(the young woman working on her social work degree),
and Arlene, the corrections officer. These are the lines I
hand out:

There are things I tell to no one. – Galway Kinnell
Heart, let us this once reason together. – Donald Justice
Imagine a man who remembers. – Patrick Lane
When you are young, every step is burning as you leave it.
   – Alison Smith
Why was that city there in the middle of my sleep? – A. F.
   Moritz
In blossom the apple tree outside ... leans in, a lover or
   confidant, with a secret to share. – Harry Thurston[17]

This exercise frees the women. Because each poem
a woman reads has been written by the group, no one
has to worry about being judged. The poems delight
them. When one woman reads a poem, another will say,
after a particular line, Yeah, that's mine. Or one woman
will say, Now that's good, and another woman will shout
out, I wrote that.

After this exercise, Rena reads a poem she wrote
earlier and the other two women say it's great and ask
if she will make copies for them. I am moved, again, by
how people in the workshops, both men and women,
cheer each other on.

University students often feel insecure when some-
one reads a strong poem. They may or may not tell the
poet they enjoyed what she wrote, but they will say to
me in one-on-one meetings that they worry they will
never be able to write as well. I have tried to reassure
students that everyone has their own journey. I tell

them it took me a long time to write poems I felt good about. I find it interesting that competition does not seem prevalent in the prison workshops.

At the end of the session, Macey sings. It is thrilling to hear her powerful, bluesy, resonant voice. I have rarely heard anyone sing this well. My impulse is to tell her how much pleasure her singing brings me and how I'd like to hear her each time I'm here. Perhaps this request would be an imposition. I have not thought it through. Nonetheless I tell her how amazing her voice is and how happy I would be if she would sing at the next session too and she says she will.

THURSDAY, MAY 29

Lynette joins us for the second session. Lynette and Macey are cousins. Lynette, a tall woman with a close-cropped afro, is older, perhaps in her early forties. She smiles when I shake her hand, says she's glad to meet me. Later the corrections officer, Arlene, says it was hard going before the workshop because Lynette got angry and called someone cunt, but Arlene decided to let her come to the workshop anyway. Lynette has a temper, she tells me.

I read the first poem, "Dedication" by Czeslaw Milosz,[18] which begins,

You whom I can not save
Listen to me.
Try to understand this simple speech as I would be
    ashamed of another.

The poem ends with the poet saying they used to put millet or poppy seeds on graves:

To feed the dead who would come disguised as birds.
I put this book here for you, who once lived
So that you should visit us no more.

I ask the women to write a poem about someone they tried to save or someone who tried to save them. Lynette says the poem is too intellectual. And it is sad. Macey says the only person she can save is herself and she is having a hard time doing that. Lynette says if she knew I would be reading sad poems she would have stayed back in the cell. Her voice sounds gruff and angry.

Perhaps I chose the wrong poem by Milosz to give out. Milosz, poet of exile, winner of the Nobel Prize, is a writer who affects me deeply. He shows, in his poems, one of love's great gifts: the revelation that all things are interconnected. His poem "Love"[19] ends,

It doesn't matter whether he knows what he serves:
Who serves best doesn't always understand.

This is a line I have repeated to myself often to help me have faith in my decisions. But his poem "Dedication" is not a success in this workshop.

I look in my satchel of poems and hand out one that was well received in the men's workshop: "How I Go to the Woods" by Mary Oliver, and ask them to write about a place that is beautiful and include who took them there. The three women say they can do that and Lynette and Macey start writing immediately.

Later I pass out poetry books I've written and the three women exclaim with enthusiasm. Lynette asks me to read the poem "Cock." I say I'll read it later.

I read "The Old Man"[20] and explain that I wrote that poem in my twenties, before I'd published any books, and put the poem away:

> *When I die the old man who lives inside me*
> *will give me his blessing*
> *and tend my body.*
>
> *I forced him to lie shivering*
> *in cold water*
> *and he forgave me.*
>
> *Eyes lively, he will oil my feet,*
> *smooth my hands.*
> *Each moment I approach death*
>
> *he grows younger, stronger.*
> *"There's so much I wanted,"*
> *I tell him. Soon, he says*
>
> *you will want nothing. When I die*
> *the old man who lives inside me*
> *will be ready and willing with answers.*
>
> *Though I, deep in his body*
> *will need no answers.*
> *I'll have no questions.*

I tell them that decades later, when I began medi-tating, I saw the old man during meditations. I say that I can ask this old man questions and he guides me without words. It took decades for my life to catch up with my poems, I say. This was one more experience that gave me faith in the power of poems: they reveal what we didn't know we knew. I put this poem in my fourth book, because it fit with other poems about Ophelia, a woman whose voice was stolen.

Macey says, The old man is taking your youth, and Lynette says, No, he is giving her something, not taking something away. But Macey reads a line from the poem: *Each moment I approach death he grows younger, stronger.* These women are very smart.

Lynette reads a piece about living with a foster family, how alone she felt. She says she is sorry it is so sad. We are all moved by what she wrote. No one says anything for a moment, but it is clear everyone in the group recognizes the depth of her pain.

Rena reads a piece about farming with her nanny. She was the only grandchild patient enough to help with the garden and felt she accomplished something when she spent time weeding. I say she must have been a big help to her grandmother. She says she loved her nanny. Macey tells us she spent more time with her granny than with her mother. She was a beautiful woman with her red-blonde hair, Macey says.

They all want to hear "Cock"[21] so I ask Arlene to read it. She says it is an honour to read a poem in front of the poet. After Arlene finishes, Lynette says, That's a great poem. And you say you don't like it.

I do like the poem, but I was embarrassed to read it because of the title.

At the end of the session Macey sings Jason Mraz's "I Won't Give Up." Then she sings a song by Adele, "We Could Have Had It All." It is thrilling listening to her. To be able to sing like that seems to me the ultimate talent. I remember one of my students at Dalhousie University said that everyone can sing. This is true and I think everyone feels happier when they allow themselves to sing. But to hear someone with such a powerful voice and always on key, this is transformative.

This is Macey's last day in the workshop as she will be released next week. She asks me to read another one of my poems and I read "Too Late,"[22] which has the lines,

> So many people
> I'll never be,
> things I won't do.
> Why list them?

Macey says, There aren't many things I haven't done! Last week, when Arlene was walking me to the exit, she told me that Macey's father makes her sell stolen goods for crack and that her mother is a prostitute. I don't know if this is gossip or fact. I can't imagine a wealthy woman, who can hire an expensive lawyer, ending up in this prison.

This is the only workshop where I have read so many of my own poems. It was not what I intended. These women and I have become colleagues, all of us sharing with each other.

WEDNESDAY, JUNE 4

Today there were only two women in the workshop, Crystal and Jenna. Jenna, in her twenties, is pale with dirty brown hair she parts in the middle. Crystal, a slender woman in her twenties as well, her long hair blonde and glossy, her skin glowing, her green eyes animated, is as glamorous as Jenna is muted.

Jenna, restless, shakes her foot as if running in

place. She says she is upset about Rena, who cannot come today because she is in the hospital. I learn later that Rena has AIDS and developed pneumonia. Jenna says she worries about Rena and wishes she could visit her. Then she says, I'm in love with her.

Crystal says, I am glad she has you, because she is on her own.

Crystal has three children. She looks so young herself, years younger than twenty-eight. She says she is an addict and that she also drinks. When she passes the liquor store she feels this deep pit in her stomach because she wants to buy liquor. She says life outside moves too fast. She is glad she is in here, because being confined might save her. There is no one outside who she feels close to. Her mother died a few years ago. Her sister, a drug addict, is also in prison.

Arlene, the corrections officer, also completes the assignment with the women. She reads a dark story about how cold her grandmother was to her. When her grandmother was dying and Arlene visited her and asked, How are you? the old woman shouted, What are you looking at?

My stepmother was like that, Crystal says. She says when she was pregnant she took good care of herself, gave up smoking, didn't want to drink. But now, when she is not in prison (and recently she was living in the outside world), everything is hazy and she wants to smoke and clear her head. She says when she was not drinking, and went into the woods, the world around her – grass, moss, trees, birds, rocks, fallen branches – came alive.

I hand out "The Gift" by Li-Young Lee.[23] Crystal says it is a hard poem and Jenna says she doesn't understand it. When I give workshops to men in the prison they are willing to guess at what a poem might mean, even if they are unsure. Women immediately assume they aren't smart enough to interpret poems. Going to difficult places in their writing is too painful for many of the women.

I read the poem again, about a father who, without causing pain, lovingly removes a splinter from his son's hand and gives it to him. The poem begins by the narrator saying his father recited a story in a gentle voice as he pulled out the splinter:

> I watched his lovely face and not the blade.
> Before the story ended, he'd removed
> the iron sliver I thought I'd die from.

When the boy becomes an adult he is able to be loving to his wife because he experienced love from his father. The poem ends,

> I did what a child does
> when he's given something to keep.
> I kissed my father.

Crystal nods and says yes, she understands the poem. We talk about how the gift his father gave him was more than gently removing a splinter. And it wasn't only love. What was bestowed on the narrator was courage to face the world. This is what love, freely given, generates. What I don't say is that the women in this room did not get the nurturing that is essential to living well. Probably because their parents were also deprived and broken.

Next we read John Terpstra's Poem "Pricked,"[24] which begins,

Funny, isn't it? I am willing to fall in love
with almost any woman that I meet,
(some more willingly than others)
as readily as others catch cold or the flu.

When they hear the first stanza, the women laugh.
Crystal rolls her eyes as if it is all too familiar.

The poem ends,

Even the women sitting in a quiet row
under the dark windows, waiting their turn
for inoculation, and old enough to be my mother –
a scary thought.

The woman I fell in love with last night
had been easing apprehensions all evening.
When she reached to prick a needle into my arm
she had so recently touched, I felt nothing.

After I read the last stanza Jenna says, Oh, so he
fell in love with the nurse because she didn't hurt him.

I ask them to write a piece about someone who
was kind to them, or unkind to them – a teacher, a
parent, a grandparent.

Crystal writes about a time she and her moth-
er, brother, and sister visited their grandmother in the
country and caught fireflies. At first her mother was
angry; her mother often got angry, Crystal says, but that
evening her anger didn't last and soon they all laughed.
It is one of the few memories she has of everyone
laughing. Mostly I didn't get along with my family, she
says, so laughing was special.

Arlene says her father can be so cruel but he is
also the greatest guy. When I ask in what way, she says
he was very loyal to her mother when her mother was
dying.

Arlene's life seems as infused with grief as those of the inmates.

After the women are brought back to their cells, Arlene says she thinks the smaller group went well. Often people go deeper and are more open in a smaller group.

WEDNESDAY, JUNE 11

When I arrive today Arlene says there will only be two people in the workshop again. Crystal is no longer here. She was released last week. This is a short-term prison so it's hard on workshops, Arlene says.

But Jenna and Lynette are here. I'm glad to see you, I say when Lynette walks in and she says she's glad to see me too. Last week Arlene did not want her to come because, Arlene explained, Lynette can be disruptive. Lynette did talk as the others were writing, but she added a lot too. Then a new person, Cassie, asks if she can come and Arlene says yes. Ruth, from the first session, joins us in the middle of class.

I ask the women to write about someone they were close to and what connects them to this person. I ask for details, what the person looks like, things they did together. I also give out the poem "Exposure" by Robin Robertson[25] to show examples of metaphor. The poem begins, *Rain, you say, is silence turned up high.* Later in the poem is the line, *Silence is rain with the sound turned down.* We talk about how alive silence can be, and sensual. Like rain, there are many kinds of silence.

In the last stanza the poet talks about seeing something left out on the line:

a life, snagged there –
drenched, shrunken,
unrecognisably mine.

How can a life be drenched, and shrunken? I ask. Do we see "life" in a new way when we compare it to the visually explicit "laundry left on a line"?

When the women start writing Arlene says, Now I'm frozen. Do you want us to use metaphor?

Only if you want to, I say. Write about someone you are close to, using any language you choose. The reason I gave examples of metaphors was to show how powerful they can be, I say.

Lynette asks how to spell "happiness."

Cassie asks how to spell "pregnant." It turns out Cassie, who is twenty, is three months pregnant. She asks, Do I have to read what I write? Only if you want to, I tell her.

Cassie asks me to read her piece, but when I can't make out her handwriting, she reads it. She writes about her mother who died of a heart attack at forty, when Cassie was seventeen. She writes that she and her mother were so close when she was growing up. They sewed together on canvas and made Christmas trees and Santas and sold what they made. She says she wishes her mom were here now. She wouldn't be proud of me being in jail, Cassie says, but she would be proud and glad that I'm pregnant. I'm a little over three months. I wish she were here to see the baby when he or she is born.

Also, my mom loved going to the bar to play the machines, Cassie writes. She writes that her grandparents died young too and she never got to meet them. She never got along with her father, who drinks a lot, and after her mother died it got so bad in her house she began living on the street.

You've had a difficult time, I say. She looks down at the floor, tears falling from her eyes down her pale cheeks. Her red hair is tied high in a ponytail, the ends tipped with orange streaks.

Ruth, the oldest inmate in the group, asks Cassie if she has anyone to help with the baby.

Cassie shakes her head. She has no brothers or sisters, just her father and her stepbrothers, but she is not speaking to them.

I ask if she has friends who can help and she shakes her head. No one asks about the father of her baby.

Perhaps there are people here who will become your friends, and who you can see when you get out, I say.

I'm here if you need someone to talk to, Ruth offers.

When Ruth volunteers to share her piece, she asks if someone else will read it. She says that will be easier for her.

Crystal tries but can't understand her writing. So I read Ruth's piece. She writes about her son Clark, the person she is closest to, she says. Clark is her oldest child and at the age of twenty-five he is becoming a remarkable young man. She talks about how he had been a thug, but now is hard-working and lives with his girlfriend and his three dogs. He puts money into her account so she can call him. He is always there for her.

She writes that her son's first name is Damon, and his middle name Clark. He prefers Clark.

Cassie interrupts and asks, Isn't Damon the name

of the devil, and Ruth says, in a matter-of-fact voice, Yes, it's the son of the devil.

She ends the piece with the sentence, I'm so very very proud to have him as my child and my best friend.

When I finish reading, Ruth is crying and Lynette and Cassie are crying too. We say how moving the piece is and how fortunate we are to have children.

Lynette says, I used to have a son like that. I ask her if her son is still alive and she says, They killed him when he was twenty-one. She is crying harder now, and puts her head in her hands. And I am crying too.

Ruth says, You know, not everyone in prison is a bad person. Some of us try hard. We've had to do things. People judge us but we're not all bad.

WEDNESDAY, JUNE 18

The next week when I go through security at the entrance of the prison the buzzer goes off, as it does every week, but today, Don, a guard I see almost every time I'm here, makes me take off my belt and boots. He is an older man and happy to talk about gardening, so today while I move through the detector I ask him about planting tomatoes. He tells me this summer has not been good for planting.

Two women come into the small entrance room after me. They are in their forties, attractive, neat. They say they are here to drop off money for their sons.

Just put it in the machine, Don says.

How does it work? one woman asks, warily looking at the big metal contraption.

It's an American machine, Don says. It should explain how it works when you begin.

My son is being transferred tomorrow, the other woman says.

I wouldn't put money in the machine if he's leaving, Don replies.

The woman looks stumped. Perhaps she hoped to be able to hand her son money.

Do you have a washroom? she asks timidly. There is a washroom a few feet away in the locked waiting room. I know this because I use it every week before I give my workshop.

No, Don says, sounding surprised by the question. This is a prison, he says.

* * *

Lynette, Crystal, Cassie, and Arlene are here.

Crystal was let out last week but now she is back with two black eyes. I don't ask what happened but she volunteers that she was jumped. What does she mean by jumped, I ask and she says people jumped her while she was waiting at the mall. I don't question why she is the one in prison if other people attacked her. Perhaps she was dealing drugs.

Crystal shows me photos of her common-law husband and her three children. They are such a handsome family and I tell her this. I only learn later that Crystal has lost custody of her children. All three are in foster care.

I give out "Happiness" by Raymond Carver[26] and ask the women to remember a time they were happy and describe the incident in detail. In the poem Carver writes about watching a boy and his friend deliver newspapers in the early morning and feels a burst of unexpected happiness:

> *for a minute*
> *death and ambition, even love,*
> *doesn't enter into this.*

Crystal says she liked poems I gave out in earlier workshops better than "Happiness." Lynette says, No, look at how he talks about the moon, referring to the line in Raymond Caver's poem,

> *The sky is taking on light,*
> *though the moon still hangs pale over the water.*

I am surprised and glad that this visual description lingers in her mind.

It is hard for Lynette to settle down. She's been nervous since the first class but today she is especially jittery. She jumps out of her chair, walks around. She seems agitated.

A new participant, Ashley, comes in late. She says that someone is always stabbing her in the back, no matter where she is. I tell her to write about that. She says Ruth, the woman who was here last week, was a rat and told on her. Told what? I don't ask. After Ruth wrote about her son, she never returned to the workshop.

I give out quotes by Thich Nhat Hanh[27] and ask each woman to read one. Cassie asks if she can read several. Yes, I say. But Crystal wants to read the ones Cassie reads. Fine, I say, I am happy to hear the lines twice.

Lynette reads, *Letting go gives us freedom, and freedom is the only condition for happiness. If, in our heart, we still cling to anything – anger, anxiety, or possessions – we cannot be free.* She says, I'm still angry at some people. Even though I know it doesn't do any good.

Crystal says, You can't just let go of anxiety. Then she reads the line, *Many people think excitement is happiness ... But when you are excited you are not peaceful. True happiness is based on peace.* Yes, she says. That's why I'm here. I want some peace.

Cassie reads, *When another person makes you suffer, it is because he suffers deeply within himself, and his suffering is spilling over. He does not need punishment; he needs help. That's the message he is sending.* She says, My first boyfriend was mean to me even when I didn't do anything to make him mad.

Thich Nhat Hanh is saying that people hurt others because they are hurt, I say. Cassie says, I don't think my boyfriend was so hurt. Then she asks if she can read the next line, *Sometimes your joy is the source of your smile, but sometimes your smile can be the source of your joy.*

Arlene says, I do find that if I smile, even when I don't feel like smiling, my mood changes and I feel better. It's like fake it 'til you make it.

Ashley reads, *To be beautiful means to be yourself. You don't need to be accepted by others. You need to accept yourself.* Nobody says a thing. I imagine we are all thinking that it is good to accept oneself, but not easy.

I read the lines, *People usually consider walking on water or on thin air a miracle. But the real miracle is not to walk either on water or on thin air, but to walk on earth. Every day we are engaged in a miracle which we don't even recognize: a blue sky, white clouds, green leaves, the black, curious eyes of a child – our own two eyes. All is a miracle.* Isn't that a fantastic quote, I say. The Bible says Jesus walked on water. But Thich Nhat Hanh says that just being alive is miraculous enough. I love the way he expresses that, I say. Then I remember that for these women, the blue sky, the white clouds can only be glimpsed behind bars.

THURSDAY, JUNE 26

Ashley, Cassie, Jenna, and Arlene are in the workshop today. I wonder if Rena is still in the hospital and if Jenna has been able to contact her, but don't ask. Crystal and Lynette are under lockdown. I don't ask how long they've been in lockdown or how long the punishment will continue. If you're in mental distress, and who in prison doesn't feel anxious, isn't lockdown – that euphemism for solitary confinement – antithetical to helping anyone?

Last year, over a thousand Canadians were placed in solitary confinement for more than fifteen days. A twenty-three-year-old Indigenous man was in segregation in a Thunder Bay, Ontario, jail, twenty-three hours a day, for four years, not able to tell day from night, his body scarred from self harm. It is hard to believe this treatment is still sanctioned, and hundreds of inmates across the country on any given day are on lockdown.[28]

Only after I stop volunteering in the prison do I read about solitary confinement and learn that in 2011, the *U.N. Special Report on Torture and Other Cruel, Inhuman or Degrading Treatment* condemned the use of solitary confinement. If it is used in exceptional circumstances, the report recommends the time period should be as short a time as possible, and the practice should never be allowed for juveniles or those with mental illness.

Today in the workshop we read the poem

"Looking at Them Asleep," by Sharon Olds.[29] Cassie and Jenna talk about how well they felt when they were pregnant and how happy they were. Jenna says she wants a baby so badly and is jealous they are all pregnant. She says she dreamed of fish swimming upstream. Yes, I think, like salmon returning to spawn. She loved being pregnant. She looks so debilitated now, her skin rough and pale, her hair brittle. Hard to imagine her healthy and strong.

The women talk about delivery at the hospital when they had their other children. Cassie says when she went to the doctor for a checkup, he said, I can't find your cervix, and she said, I know I have one! Everyone in the workshop has had several children except Cassie, who is pregnant with her first.

Cassie says she didn't think she could have a baby. Her mother didn't think she was fertile either, until Cassie was born, and Cassie was a surprise.

Not much scientific thinking here, Ashley says.

I give them the poem "What Saves Us" by Bruce Weigl[30] and ask what they think he means by, *We are not always right about what we think will save us.*

Ashley says she does not understand the poem but when I ask her to read it again, out loud, she does understand it. Often it takes several readings to comprehend a poem, I say, and even when we don't grasp it entirely, something about the poem can touch us and ring true. Besides, the question about what will actually save us and what we think will save us is challenging. Weigl ends the poem with these lines:

> *People die sometimes so near to you*
> *you feel them struggling to cross over,*
> *the deep untangling, of one body from another.*

We talk about how we are all connected to one another, though the connection isn't always obvious. In the first workshop, Ruth and Macey were moved by Rena's poem and this made Rena happy. Earlier, Ruth offered to help Cassie take are of her baby after the baby is born. Our words, our actions, our moods affect everyone we interact with.

Cassie, the least interested in the poem, writes two poems about the baby she is going to have. She loves the baby who will be born in six months, she writes. They will always be there for each other. Both poems have the title *BABY!*

Afterwards I accompany Arlene to her office where she is going to photocopy something for the next workshop. An inmate there says her mother only has a cell phone so she can't call collect. She says she heard there is a way to call from one of the offices. An officer in the room says, I've never heard tell, and Arlene says she will try to find out more. I marvel at the distance between a workshop where there is so much excitement about motherhood, to an encounter where the system makes it difficult even to speak to one's mother.

Poetry – the language to foment revolution
– Dr. Erin Wunker[31]

Our bodies do not all look the same. Our lived experiences are not the same. Some of us have more privilege and some of us have less. How, then, do we carry this collective gathering into the future in ethical ways? How do we build collective, allied, and coalitional means of resisting oppressions, especially when those oppressions will get read onto our bodies and written on our skins differently? ...

I've been thinking about the language of resistance.

I've been thinking about what language we can use to speak collective resistance when the "we" is not necessarily collective.

I've been thinking about how one can stand in solidarity with others without trying to overshadow or co-opt someone else's cause as their own.

What language do we use to refuse what is and imagine what could be?

For me, a teacher and student of literature, that language is the language of poetry.

Poetry can, I think, move us from where we are into where we could be, even if "we" don't experience the world in the same way.

Poetry is, I think, the language at the root of political action. Poetry requires that we shift our frames of reference, squint our eyes to see the poet's message more clearly, or listen with our whole bodies as the poet speaks. Poetry might not be the language of policy change, but can, I think, be the language to foment revolution.

(From Erin Wunker's talk at the Halifax March to support the Women's March on Washington. She is an assistant professor in the Department of English, Dalhousie University.)

CHAPTER FIVE

By now I know the drill. Each week I park my car in the visitors' lot, ring the buzzer on the outside door to the prison, and when a voice asks why I am here I say, Writing Workshop. They buzz me in. Then I wait in the room that has a scanner I must walk through so the guards can make sure I am not carrying contraband.

The room has a little window and I look through to see what the guards are doing. Sometimes a guard is talking on the phone while another is working at a computer or eating his lunch. Some days I can't see anyone, as guards are in the office further back. I wait. Then I look through the window again to see if they've returned. Often, they're in the room but do not buzz me through. I move away from the window. I sigh.

Finally someone opens the door for me. One guard says, You know, you are very impatient. It's true. Every week I am eager for the guards to open the door so I can go through the metal detector, sign in, lock my handbag and coat in the locker, put on the bullet-proof vest, and get to the workshop, where the time always seems too brief. I promise the guards I will be more patient.

I mention to the social work student who works with me in the East Wing that the guards accused me of having no patience. She says, The guards feel they are doing you a favour and they want to be appreciated. They don't want their job to be harder because of you. You have to suck up to them.

Each week, as I continue to show up, the guards are friendlier, smiling when they say hello. These guys are in prison five days a week for long hours, eating lunch at their desk, walking down the windowless corridors. Even though they've chosen to be here, nonetheless, here is where they are. They want to make very clear that they are different from the men they guard, whereas I don't have to make that distinction. I don't believe I am that different from the prisoners, except that I have been luckier. I've had more opportunities.

The guards buzz me through the second and third series of doors and I make my way through the maze of corridors to the room where I will be meeting with men from the West Wing. West Wing supposedly holds more "hardened criminals."

THURSDAY, JULY 3

Savannah is the corrections officer in this group. She is in her early thirties, tall and curvaceous, her body strong, her tanned skin luminous, her light brown hair thick and tied in a ponytail. Many of the female corrections officers I have met in the prison are young and attractive, in charge of men who are also young. I wonder how she and other women deal with unwanted sexual attention that is bound to cause tension, but I do not ask. I wonder if this is addressed by the administration.

I hand out the poem "Desiderata."[32] The poem

sounds as if it were written centuries ago, a mistake compounded when it was published with devotional material for a church which included the church's founding date, 1692. However, the poem was actually written in the early twentieth century by Max Erhmann. When my children were young, friends of mine from Quaker Meeting, Margery and Ray, had the poem printed on a plaque and gave it to all the members of our weekly meeting. My family loved it. In all the prison workshops I've given, both men and women respond strongly and positively to "Desiderata" as well. I see a faint smile on Justin's face when I look up, after I read the following lines:

> *Nurture strength of spirit to shield you in sudden*
> *misfortune. ...*
> *Beyond a wholesome discipline,*
> *be gentle with yourself.*

Justin, a young white man with dark hair in a buzz cut, keeps rubbing the inside of his arm. Are those needle marks I see? He says, That was deep, after I finish reading the poem.

Collin reads the line, *Avoid loud and aggressive persons; they are vexations to the spirit,* and says, coldly, but, it seems to me, defensively – I'm aggressive. Collin, a handsome Black man in his late twenties, early thirties, holds his body rigidly and I've seen him glare at other participants. He is very controlled and, I imagine, controlling.

We talk about the line, *Do not distress yourself with imaginings. Many fears are born of fatigue and loneliness.* Justin says he worries about things all the time.

But it doesn't help, does it? Samuel says. Samuel is

a slim, tall, young man in his early twenties. He is gentle and handsome, sporting a magnificent afro, his skin a pale russet brown. His voice is soothing.

I ask these guys to write about what they love and what they hate about morning, afternoon, evening. This is an introductory assignment and does not produce interesting responses. It's a delicate balance, deciding what assignments to give first to relax participants and develop trust. I am slowly learning.

MONDAY, JULY 14

I had to miss Thursday's workshop as there was a prison shutdown. I come the following Monday and say I am sorry I had to miss the Thursday workshop. Samuel says he was sorry too that I wasn't there. Today Samuel seems down. Savannah tells me his trial is on Friday. He is charged with murder. I find this hard to believe. He is so kind to the other guys, telling them when he especially likes one of their pieces. Two of the men in the original workshop, Jamil and Dalton, both in their thirties, do not return, but another man comes.

Collin, who has a deep, sonorous voice, reads the poem "Quickthorn," by Siobhán Campbell[33] after I read it.

I ask them what they think haw means, a word she uses throughout the poem:

> Don't bring haw into the house at night
> or in any month with a red fruit in season
> or when starlings bank against the light,
> don't bring haw in.

Savannah, the corrections officer in the group, says it means death.

Collin thinks haw means her, the other woman. It could certainly be that, I say. Poems, if they are good, have many layers and various interpretations. They are spacious enough for the reader to bring his or her life into the poem, I tell them.

I say that when I read the poem to Luke, my twenty-four-year-old son, he said he thought haw referred to hem and haw. Don't bring confusion and indecision into the house (and into our relationship) was the way Luke read haw and Samuel thinks that is a good interpretation. Haw can also refer to hawthorn, I say, a tree that is poisonous. Jealousy, ambivalence, suspicion are all poisonous.

I ask them to look at the language in the poem and point out how "plucked" and "thumb" echo the same "u" sound, and how this technique is called assonance, which can be found throughout the poem. Alliteration is another technique the poet used. Both meld the poem into a cohesive piece. The men point out examples of alliteration: haw, house, hidden; thwart, thumb; low and lilting. They identify examples of assonance: haw/long; green/field; lilting/bring/in. We talk about how satisfying it is to hear a sound echoed, especially when the letters that produce the sound are different.

Then the men read the homework they did, describing a time they were happy. Samuel reads his piece about playing with his brother when he was young. He has a twin brother and I want to know what it is like to be a twin. I ask him if he could write more about his brother and he says he will. Justin writes about spending a day with his father, playing golf. He was going to live with his father and then he got arrested. Collin writes about what freedom would feel like. Devon does not do the exercise.

Justin reads a rap poem and talks about how sweet revenge is. I tell him I disagree. Samuel says, There is closure in revenge, but I say revenge just perpetuates the cycle for more revenge. I say, I think only forgiving offers freedom. I hope I don't sound like I am preaching, I say, but the power of compassion is healing whereas revenge is bitter and destructive. Have they ever been forgiven by someone they harmed, and doesn't that make them want to pay forward that kindness?

I tell the men that I listen to *This American Life* on Sunday night at midnight on CBC. Do they have radios in the prison? Yes, they say.

Radio One or Two? Collin asks.

CBC Radio One, I say, and tell them the program this week was about a boy in middle school, who everyone made fun of, a boy who did not wash, whose clothes were always filthy, and who was constantly angry. Then the teacher explained that the hot water in this young man's house was turned off. She said to her students, You have someone to take care of you, make sure there is food in the house. He doesn't have that. The students began being kind to the boy and the change their kindness had on the boy was dramatic.[34]

I ask how compassion can help us and we go around the room, each man talking about an instance of compassion that affected him. Samuel says his grandmother would invite kids in for lunch when she knew they had no place to go. Afterwards Samuel asks if I am a Buddhist. I say no, but I like the Buddhist philosophy. He says he read *The Power of Now* by Eckhart Tolle. I liked that book too, I tell him, and he says he thought I would.

Justin asks what my credentials are and I tell him I teach in the creative writing program at Dalhousie University and have a few books of poetry published. They ask me to read a poem of mine and I recite "Not in the Warm Earth,"[35] as it is a poem I know from memory. I tell them I wrote it after I had a dream that I was on a raft with my parents and they fell off the raft and I could not save them. I said it was a powerful dream because it reminded me we are all in the same boat. Some get off earlier, some stay on longer, but we are all navigating unpredictable water.

That's deep, Samuel says. The poem has the lines,

In the middle of the night
they wake me. They tell me they're worried. I've made
    mistake
after mistake.

When I recite that line, Collin says, That's strong.

After class Savannah thanks me for having patience with Justin, who seemed addled with drugs.

THURSDAY, JULY 17

The assignment for the men was to write about their fathers, and to include dialogue. I asked if they could do that and they said yes. But they do not do this. I ask if it was difficult to write about their fathers and they say no, they just didn't have time during the week. But the following Thursday Savannah has to cancel because she is sick and the next time I see them is two weeks later. No one has written about his father.

When I gave the assignment to third-year university students, they wrote intimate poems about either their mother or father. But the assignment is not successful in prison. It is not difficult to imagine that many do not have close relationships with their fathers.

This week I ask the men to write freestyle for ten minutes beginning with, "It's not true that ..." Devon and Collin would not read theirs. Samuel wrote that it is not true that fog is depressing. He tells how he loves walking down foggy roads, being invisible, imagining a different world than the one he is in. He talks about the effect music has when he listens as he is walking in a dense mist, over a bridge, the fog closing behind him so he cannot see where he just was.

The mood is striking and the idea of writing about fog is surprising. The men say they like the piece and I do too. I correct some misspelled words and run-on sentences when I type it. Then I send it to the student who started the literary journal. I hope she gets back to me soon.

THURSDAY, JULY 24

That next week, while I am waiting for the guard to open the inner door, I do not look through the little window to let the guards know I want to be admitted. Instead I read the notices on the wall:

NO CELL PHONES PAGERS BLACKBERRIES ETC. BEYOND THIS POINT EXCEPT INSTITUTION CELL PHONES USED FOR OFFENDER ESCORTS AND STORED AT THE MAIN DESK.

They still do not open the door. I keep reading:

ALL VISITORS ENTERING THE FACILITY WILL BE SUBJECTED TO SEARCH. VISITORS MUST WALK THROUGH THE METAL DETECTOR PRIOR TO ENTRANCE TO THE FACILITY. SHOULD THE METAL DETECTOR BE ACTIVATED VISTIORS MAY BE REQUIRED TO SUBMIT TO HAND HELD DETECTOR SEARCH BY STAFF. REFUSAL MAY RESULT IN VISITORS NOT GAINING ENTRANCE TO FACILITY.

Finally one of the guards lets me in. I say, I have been more patient, haven't I? and he nods and says, You have been more patient, Carole.

In a few weeks one of the guards will tell me he fishes mackerel and will offer to bring me fresh fish. We smile at each other. I am getting in the guards' good books. I am beginning to enjoy seeing them as well.

WEDNESDAY, JULY 30

Samuel, Collin, and Justin come to the workshop and a new participant, Ben, who is only eighteen and shy. The assignment I give is to take the line "Though I try to hide it" and continue from there. Ben writes about trying to hide his feelings for a woman who was older than him. Everyone in the group tells him they like the piece. Samuel's piece begins, "Though I try to hide it, I like to smile." The men and I agree this line is powerful because it is surprising.

They also bring in an assignment about a place they like to go. Samuel reads a poem he wrote about a candy store. He loves candy. The poem has very basic rhymes, and I say, If participants write a poem again, I'd like them to challenge themselves by writing a poem that does not rhyme. I explain that I ask this of my students at Dal as well for the first few assignments. I ask if anyone might tell me why I make this suggestion. No one responds. I say, Often beginning poets reach for the easiest rhyme and sacrifice meaning. Choosing a word just because it rhymes is often less demanding than trying to formulate a more authentic and surprising description. Samuel says, Yeah, you found me out. I didn't work hard on this.

I tell him I am so glad he is open to suggestions. That week the student who started the journal emails to tell me she has accepted Samuel's piece about fog. I email Savannah with the news and tell her we need a few lines of biography from Samuel. Also, the editor wants to omit Samuel's last sentence in the piece. I ask if I can pick up the bio at the next workshop. I say it is unusual that a piece written so quickly is accepted. I hope this inspires Samuel to keep writing.

Savannah sends me the following email:

```
Wow that is great news! I am
heading up to the dayroom now.
I look forward to his expres-
sion when I tell him! I will let
him know about the last line and
bio. Thanks Carole! I will see
you tomorrow around 1:40 pm.
```

I can't wait to see Samuel and congratulate him.

WEDNESDAY, AUGUST 6

When I see Samuel the following week, although he already knows his piece will be published, I tell him again for the pleasure of seeing him smile. He says, Thank you so much. He asks if there are further courses he can take and I say he might want to get his GED here.

He already got his GED at another prison, he tells me. He is only twenty-three and has already been in more than one prison?

In his bio he did not want to say he is an inmate. I tell him that in my opinion it would be good to include that because, first, it's honest, and, second, it will give people a different view of what a prisoner is. He says he likes that view. Also, as my husband points out later when I tell him about this quandary, He'll make more of an impact with that in his bio.

When I tell Samuel he has a lot of talent and I hope he will continue writing, he thanks me and smiles his shy smile. Then he says, I don't like writing, though!

Welcome to the world of writing, I want to say. I wanted to quote Thomas Mann, who said, "A writer is somebody for whom writing is more difficult than it is for other people,"[36] but at the time I wasn't sure whose words those were.

These are a few sentences from Samuel's bio: Samuel was born in Halifax in 1991. He has a twin brother. When he was seventeen he won a poetry award in his school. Samuel is currently in the Central Nova Scotia Correctional Facility.

WEDNESDAY, AUGUST 13

In the final workshop Collin asked for another first line other than "Though I try to hide it ..." I give him the line "It's true that ..." and he writes a political piece about the U.S. It is a conventional piece of political beliefs and though I agree with his views, there is nothing original here and Collin's voice is lost in dogma and in rehashing what has been said many times by others. The week before he disagreed with me when I quoted Thich Nhat Hanh about everyone being related. He sees the world as inherently in conflict, perpetually divided into factions and territories that need to be defended against enemies.

Collin looks older than he is. He is such a handsome young man, his face symmetrical and strong with a square jaw. I wonder if he is aware of his good looks. I wonder too why he is so detached and cut off. I am passionate about the poems I hand out. Does he view me as an overly emotional teacher?

Afterward I say to Savannah, Collin is very distant in these workshops. He doesn't reveal much about himself.

She says, He is pretty high up in the gang world and wants to maintain his aloofness.

I say, That's scary. Do you ever get scared?

Yes! this young correctional officer with a two-year-old at home tells me. You have to be crazy not to feel a bit scared some of the time, she says.

WEDNESDAY, AUGUST 20

Today we have a new participant, Mason, a white man in his twenties. Savannah tells me that Ben and Mason are brothers. Their father is out of the picture. They were brought up by their grandmother, a church-going woman.

If there is one thing the men in prison have in common, they are poor. If you are rich, you do not end up in the Central Nova Scotia Correctional Facility, or not for long.

I ask the men if they would consider coming in next session with a song they could sing. Mason says he does not know many songs, mostly church songs. I'd like to hear a church song, I tell him.

I ask them to do something kind this week for someone and tell me about it next week. It doesn't have to be a large gesture, just something that will make someone feel better about their day. I say I will try to do that too.

Justin says, What do you mean "try"? You come here, that's a good deed.

I smile at Justin. He's generous to say this. I wonder if the men know how much I learn from them. I should tell them but this doesn't feel like the right time to say it. I don't want to offer a compliment for a compliment. Perhaps this is an error in judgement.

I ask the guys to write for ten minutes, beginning with the line "I try not to." Collin writes about trying not to act on his anger. Ben writes that he tries not to fail. Anger helps him not to fail, he says. I ask how he defines failure and he says, That is not what the piece is about. I try to explain that he did talk about failure and he says, I talked about how not to fail.

Samuel says, You *do* have to define failure because you're talking about failure. Ben says, The judge says I have to change, but this is just how I feel. I'm not going to change. I write how I feel.

I say, If you can put into words what you mean by failure, what you think failure is, that will be helpful to the reader, and to you too, I think.

He repeats, This is not about failure.

You are taking the easy way out, I sigh. As soon as I say this I feel bad. Isn't there a better way to deal with this than to criticize him? He is only eighteen. I have to have more patience than this, if I want to be helpful. I have to let things go and not hammer a point home.

We read Sharon Olds' "Looking at Them Asleep." We talk about how powerful the last line is because it presents, in a new way, something that has been written about many times. The poet describes looking at her sleeping children and writes,

... oh my Lord how I
know these two. When love comes to me and says
What do you know, I say, This girl, this boy.

We talk about what personification means and how effectively the poet personified love.

Ben does not make eye contact. He is looking down at the table. I apologize and tell him I did not mean to make him feel bad. He says, You didn't make me feel bad.

Later I ask what emotion is stronger than anger. No one says anything. I say, Love. It is so powerful. We will do so much for someone we love. So, I'd like to end this workshop session by saying your name, with love, Samuel, Ben, Justin, Mason, Collin, Savannah. Then I plow on: When we feel this love, we understand life is sacred and we can't harm anyone.

Later I tell Savannah I hope I didn't sound too preachy and she says I didn't sound preachy but she doesn't think the guys are going to get that life is sacred.

WEDNESDAY, AUGUST 27

Justin, Collin, Ben, and Mason are here. Samuel comes late because he is in a meeting with his lawyer.

I give out quotes by Rumi[37] and each of the men reads a quote. Ben reads: *In your light I learn how to love. In your beauty, how to make poems. You dance inside my chest where no one sees you, but sometimes I do, and that sight becomes this art.* Then he says, That's beautiful.

Later Samuel reads that quote and says, I don't understand it. I thank Samuel for sharing that he doesn't know what Rumi means and the men discuss the quote. Mason says, Inspiration is something you can feel inside. It's like that joy you feel in your chest when you're in love, I say.

Ben also reads the quote, *There is a candle in your heart, ready to be kindled. There is a void in your soul, ready to be filled. You feel it, don't you?* and Ben says again, That's beautiful.

I give out a certificate to Collin and Justin who are both leaving. Collin will be going to a long-term prison. He wrote, in the in-class session when I asked people to begin with "I want," that he wanted to get out in 2017 at his first parole. He is so young and has already spent four years in jail with many more years ahead. He is here for robbery, not murder.

Darren, who has not attended the workshop before, wants a certificate. Look at all this writing I did, he says, and shows me pages of rap. I say the certificates are for those who come for six weeks.

Darren keeps insisting that he needs the certificate. It will look good for the probation officers, he says. I try to explain that the purpose of the course isn't for the certificate, but to learn and share. He keeps asking and finally I say, This is boring. Let's move on.

But the fact is, there are few programs and little funding for programs where inmates can learn about themselves and what they love. In this six-week workshop the men share so much.

I look at Samuel, who is so thoughtful. I was told by one of the corrections officers that he and another man are accused of murder. When she tells me the story, I remember hearing it on the news, months before. The story was grizzly and shocking. I wondered if this was a drug deal gone wrong.

Before I knew any of the men involved, I thought of the accused as monsters. But the Samuel I know is so much more than the crime he committed. As John Edgar Wideman says in one of his short stories, "The facts speak for themselves, but never speak for us."[38]

More than a year after the last workshop, when I am at home listening to the radio, I hear a news announcement that Samuel has been convicted of murder and sentenced to life. The announcement rips through me. Listening to the news I think, The heart of the story is missing. I feel so much grief. Samuel seemed like a relative whose disregarded life and experiences few would get to know.

Jails prove we have failed each other again and again.

How do we help those in need? It is a crucial question because isn't this the only way we can save each other?

From a report in the *National Post*:[39]

More than half of Canadian adults in jail
were awaiting trial rather than serving sentences
in 2014 and 2015.

No one would want to be **"warehoused"**
even for a single day in one of Canada's **"crowded,
violent, disturbing"** remand centres
that prisoners call **"the buckets."**

Latimer said, "If you're behind bars,
whether you're presumed innocent
or not, whether it's for
30 days or 90 days, it can be a problem.

"People can **lose their rent,**
... **their employment,**
... **their housing** because they're *not able
to interact with the world.*"

*(Aileen Donnelly spoke with Catherine Latimer,
executive director of the John Howard Society.)*

According to information released by Halifax Regional Police[40]

Black people three times more likely
to be street checked than white
individuals. No wait. Black people street checked

six times more than white people
in Halifax. New report doubles
2017 estimate. Odds are highest for Black

men. Then Arab males. Then Black females.
Nearly two-thirds – 61 per cent –
of people checked had **no prior criminal** charges.

"People will automatically assume
that the reason why there's a disparity
is because of racial profiling." Halifax Regional

Police chief in 2017. He says more analysis is needed
to determine what the numbers mean,
and whether officers will need more

training about racial profiling. Police Chief confirmed
that at no time in 11 years
of collecting statistics on street checks

did anyone
with Halifax Regional Police
analyze the data.

From a 1962 interview with Dr. Martin Luther King and reporter Eleanor Fischer in Atlanta.[41]

EF: Were you aware during this period of the problems that faced Negros in the South ...?

MLK: Oh yes. I became aware of these problems, first, I believe, when I was about five years old. I was raised and grew up on Auburn Avenue in Atlanta and in front of our house was a store and this store was owned and operated by one of the white citizens of Atlanta. They had two or three children and we were about the same age. When we were three and four we played together. And this was not an unusual thing. But I never will forget when the day came that my playmates, my inseparable playmates just found excuses and refused to play with us. My brother was concerned about this, he was a year younger, and I was very much concerned. This continued for a week or two and I started talking to my mother about it and for the first time I came to see the problems because she tried to explain the best way she could to a child that's five years old the problems which Negroes confronted in the South as a result of the legacy of slavery and then segregation.

EF: It must be a very difficult job for any mother, I wonder if any mother really can explain this to a child ...

MLK: Well, it's almost impossible to thoroughly explain it. It seems to me that the only thing that the mother can do, the Negro mother, is try from the beginning to instil in the child a sense of somebodyness. This is what my mother tried to do. She made it very clear that in spite of these conditions you are as good as anybody else and you must not feel that you are not. This was her way of saying you should not have an inferiority complex. This is very difficult because even though you say this, in words, it is very difficult for the child not to develop, unconsciously, this sense of inferiority because he lives every day in the midst of a system which stares him in the face saying you're less than, you're not equal to. And the tendency is to develop this sense of inferiority because of the existence of the system.

Why succeeding against the odds can make you sick.[42]

James Hamblin's 2017 article discusses Dr. Gene Brody's work in African-American communities in rural Georgia. The public-health researcher "focuses on people who overcome the odds to prosper, academically, professionally and financially." Resilient traits are needed to achieve success against overwhelming odds: Such strivers "cultivate persistence, set goals and work diligently toward them, navigate setbacks, focus on the long term, and resist temptations that might knock them off course."

One would think such traits and activities are desirable and that achievement of upward mobility would result in improvements in health. But decades of research finds that "when resilient people work hard within a system that has not afforded them the same opportunities as others, their physical health deteriorates."

The article goes on to describe what Dr. Sherman James called "the John Henryism scale," which identifies people who employ great effort to cope with challenges. "The scale is based on how strongly people identify with statements like 'When things don't go the way I want them to, that just makes me work even harder' and 'I've always felt that I could make of my life pretty much what I wanted to make of it.' He found that high scores correlated with worse health among poor and working-class Blacks. Notably, like Dr. Brody, Dr. James found that working-class white Americans seemed unaffected by this phenomenon.

"Constantly bathing cells in stress hormones, the science would suggest, could sponsor more inflammatory responses," Dr. Brody explains. He makes clear that such stress can lead to diabetes and other autoimmune disorders.

"Because African-Americans experience so much more exclusion and degradation – something that working-class whites didn't experience at the time – that probably created conditions that were ripe for us to only see the effects in Blacks," James said about his research in the '80s.

Board awards nearly $600,000 for racist discrimination[43]

"... Last year, [Lynn] Connors [chair of the Nova Scotia Human Rights Commission board] found widespread racial discrimination and a poisoned work environment at Halifax Transit's garage.

"... The complainant is white, but his wife is African Nova Scotian, and black and Indigenous co-workers also suffered under the actions of a former co-worker.

"... The mechanic filed the complaint with the human rights commission over 12 years ago, in July 2006, saying he suffered from trauma due to the hostile workplace.

"In her 2018 ruling, Connors said the complainant had been frightened and terrorized.

"Allegations in the case included a message scrawled on the men's bathroom wall, which said 'all minorities not welcome; show you care, burn a cross.' It was signed by 'a member of the Baby Hitler.'"

(by Keith Doucette, The Canadian Press)

CHAPTER SIX

SEPTEMBER 17

As I drive to the prison to begin another writing workshop on the North Wing, I am thinking about something that happened in my class at Dalhousie the previous week. One of the students missed the first three classes and last week was her first class. I was wary of letting her take the course, as it is hard to catch up on three writing assignments. But she'd emailed and asked for the assignments, which I'd sent her, and today she handed them all in. In class, she responded to questions with such intelligence and passion, she trembled as she spoke. When I said, That's such a perceptive response, she blushed with pleasure. She is a thin, pretty woman about twenty years old, with spiky black hair, many earrings around the curve of her ear, and a nose ring. Whenever I say to my husband that a student is pretty, he repeats the words he knows my father said when I was a teenager: All young people are beautiful. I disagreed with my father then, but now I see how true this is.

After class the young woman came to my office to find out if she'd missed anything when she was absent. I told her I was very glad to have her in the class. Again she blushed as if not used to compliments. When she took off her sweater, both her arms had raw red welts, scarred from forearm to wrist from slashing.

When I was in my twenties I had a friend who slashed her arms with razors to distract herself from deeper pain. Being young can be difficult. I am glad this young woman is taking the class. It would have been wrong to deny her permission because she'd missed a few classes. And yet I came close to doing just that.

There are always students in my university classes who write poems only they can write. Their work is immediate and surprising. They face their own fear and write with great emotional depth. It is thrilling to work with these students. When they critique poems by classmates, many see things I haven't seen. I admire such intelligence and energy.

But of course there are students who don't read assignments, who write poems that are predictable, who repeat second-hand observations they've heard or read.

I try to explain that unless the poet learns something from a poem, the reader will learn nothing. Poems are not essays written to persuade, they're discoveries, or, as Yeats said, "Out of the quarrel with others we make rhetoric; out of the quarrel with ourselves we make poetry."[44]

I say that if there is something in the poem that embarrasses the poet, that is often a sign the subject is powerful and I encourage students to explore it.

The challenge is to be supportive and encouraging to all students, and at the same time to offer meaningful critiques. So often I feel guilty about not giving enough critical critiques. On the other hand, I want to empower students to have the confidence to work harder and go deeper. I emphasize that student critiques must focus on the poem, not the poet, and that criticism should help the poet write a stronger poem. It is a challenge to balance support and critical appraisal.

During the first few classes, when we talk about the power of poetry and read poems from *The Norton Anthology*, students share my excitement about poetry and I leave class feeling great. However, once we start critiquing student work, especially poems that are weak, I wonder, have I said too much? Have I said enough? Have I been too enthusiastic to one student, making my lack of enthusiasm for another's work too obvious? And then I am required to give students marks, which complicates things further.

Working in the prison, I am only here to encourage. And participants don't write poems, but paragraphs about their experience. I may make a suggestion, but I never give a line by line critique. To encourage people is always satisfying, especially when those I praise have received such little acknowledgement for their strengths and are often not aware of their talents, not least of which is surviving a system that can be brutally dismissive.

Yet in the last workshops I gave at the prison, I was impatient with Ben. I wonder if I can do better with the new group of men on the North Wing.

CHAPTER SEVEN

WEDNESDAY, SEPTEMBER 17

At the first workshop, again on the North Wing, I give out the poem "The Legend," by Garrett Hongo[45], to the six men participating: Warren, Kenny, Travis, Wesley, Emery, and Preston. The poem is about a man who is shot by *a boy – that's all he was.* The man shot is

> *Asian, Thai or Vietnamese,*
> *and very skinny, dressed as one of the poor*
> *in rumpled suit pants and a plaid mackinaw*
> *dingy and too large.*

The poem ends,

> *Let the night sky cover him as he dies.*
> *Let the weaver girl cross the bridge of heaven*
> *and take up his cold hands.*

Then I ask the men to tell me where they are from and a little about themselves, and if they want, what they think of the poem. Warren, from a First Nations community, says of the ending, That's cool. I agree. When I repeat his words he says, No, I said, that's deep.

He says the myth at the end brings comfort. His culture too has legends that are helpful. He has six children, the oldest twenty. I say he doesn't look old enough to have a twenty-year-old son and he smiles and thanks me.

Travis tells the group that he overcame cancer, that he is a warrior, a fighter. I talk about kindness and forgiveness as being tools of a warrior. Do I sound like some self-righteous Mother Superior? I hope not. Warren asks if I am a psychologist. They ask if I have books published. I say I do and I will bring them in.

Kenny, a man in his early thirties who grew up in Halifax, doesn't say much.

Wesley is also in his thirties. He lets us know his wife is as guilty as he is but he is taking the rap for her so she can be home with their kids. However, she did not visit him last week and he is pissed.

Emery is originally from Winnipeg but moved to Nova Scotia when he was in grade school. He does not speak much during the workshop.

Preston, a man in his fifties, lives in Yarmouth. He was working for Lowell, an elderly man in Yarmouth. It's so surprising to hear Preston mention Lowell's name. I know Lowell as well because he was friends with Ray and Marge, who held Quaker Meetings at their house.

I used to go to Quaker Meeting on Sundays, and sit in silence for an hour with other Friends. Outside roosters would crow; Marge and Ray had chickens and roosters. In Meeting, no one speaks during silent worship, unless the spirit moves them. Afterwards, before we shared potluck lunch, we talked briefly about how the silence affected us. I was always moved when Ray or Marge spoke. They were in their seventies when I first went to meeting, and their words came from a deep place. I remember Ray saying how much he missed his children now that they were grown, living far from home with their own families. He talked about the pleasure he had whenever he spent time with them. I met Lowell through Marge and Ray. Six degrees of separation.

In the discussion of Garrett Hongo's "The Legend," the poem about a man who is *dressed as one of the poor,* we talk about poverty, disparity of income, how and why some people have fewer options than others. Kenny says he has never been able to stay at a job. But so many people in prison haven't had a chance to develop their strengths. I agree with psychologists who say drugs are not the problem, they are a symptom of the problem. Abuse, oppression, racism, a history of slavery are not easily overcome. What causes the pain a drug user is trying to suppress?

When the word "failure" and "failing" come up, I am reminded of a recent conversation I had with Marie, a woman in her late seventies, who lives alone down the road from us. She came over for lunch the other day and I described walking Whimsy, our fifteen-year old golden retriever. Walking Whimsy is like practising walking meditation, as she will often stop and refuse to budge. I told Marie that I have to pet Whimsy and scratch her ears and tell her I love her before she will proceed to walk a little further, only to stop again a few minutes later. Marie said, She is failing and wants love. When Bill heard this, he said, speaking in Whimsy's imagined voice, What! Failing? I didn't know you could pass or fail in this game.

But for these men the price to pay for mistakes, for failing, is high, marking their lives forever.

WEDNESDAY, SEPTEMBER 24

When I drive to the prison and buzz the front door they will not let me in. The prison has been shut down for two days and no one notified me. I am impatient and angry. Why didn't the corrections officer call to let me know and save me the long drive? Avery, a young woman taking a degree in social work and doing her practicum at the prison, and who will join the workshop when it gets underway, is not here to tell me not to take these things personally, that the CO has other responsibilities and I am not a high priority. And I do not yet have the Eckhart Tolle CD *The Power of One* from the library, which I will get a few weeks later, and which I will listen to as I drive: "Always say 'yes' to the present moment ... Surrender to what is. Say 'yes' to life – and see how life suddenly starts working for you rather than against you."[46] This will help on future occasions.

WEDNESDAY, OCTOBER 1

I give out two poems by Li-Young Lee, "Eating Together" and "Eating Alone."[47] The poem "Eating Alone" ends,

> White rice steaming, almost done. Sweet green peas
> fried in onions. Shrimp braised in sesame
> oil and garlic. And my own loneliness.
> What more could I, a young man, want.

In "Eating Together," Li-Young Lee describes eating with his family. The presence of his father, who had died, is powerfully evoked. The poem ends,

Then he lay down
to sleep like a snow-covered road
winding through pines older than him,
without any travelers, and lonely for no one.

Kenny complains that these poems are no good. They are about death. Wesley says they don't rhyme. He doesn't like them. Doug says they are deep, and death is part of life.

These poems are emotionally resonant for me, but I have done nothing to prepare these men for Li-Young Lee's words and I can understand why several of the men are not ready to immerse themselves in the poems.

I return to an assignment I'd given in other workshops and that was successful. I ask the men to write about a place they went that is special to them and who took them there. I say I want many details so that I will recognize the place if I go there.

Emery writes about fly fishing, how it is different than trout fishing, how he used to spend hours waiting for the salmon. Then each fisherman would move downstream so another could stand where he stood. Emery says, It's fairer that way. You have to slide the rod over to catch the fish.

Wesley writes that when he was five his grandfather put him in a basket and lifted it up with a winch. He dangled the basket over the water, where fisherman were bringing in tuna. The boy was terrified and his grandfather laughed! Wesley sees nothing wrong with this scene.

Another writes about being at peace after skiing. I praise these writings. Travis says, That was fantastic, about the pieces the guys read. Travis writes something more vague, about life, death, pain.

For homework I ask them to write about a meal they had, in prison or outside of prison, alone or with family. Describe a meal they remember and why they remember it. But at the next class no one has done his homework assignment. I ask the men if they still want me to give them assignments to do during the week and they say they do.

WEDNESDAY, OCTOBER 8

I hand out the poem "Sounds" by Howard Altmann.[48] We talk about the power of sound and how sound works in the last stanza. The poet talks about a man who writes a poem for a woman and after she listens,

> *her silence will begin to drop its sounds*
> *The way rain does not hurry*
> *to cover all that is ground.*
> *The way a horizon gradually recovers*
> *from the passing of a train.*

I speak about how clarifying feelings and thoughts in writing helps to better understand one's actions in everyday life.

This may be an audacious claim, I say, but I believe it is true.

Then I ask them to write a letter to their six-year-old selves, telling, in detail, how wonderful this little boy was and the good things that are in store for him. Even though they are incarcerated, they won't be here forever.

Kenny, who gave me such a hard time last week, telling me he didn't like the poems I brought in, tells me he is happy to be here. He is on methadone, which may be why he was so irritable last week.

He does not share the letter he writes to his six-year-old self. Wesley writes to his two-year-old son as he can not remember much about his childhood.

The assignment I give this week is to write about someone the men thought they did not like, but end up liking. Or write about a situation they thought would be dismal but turned out to be a good experience. Write about a situation that was unexpected, I say.

Wesley says he will write about his mother. He hasn't spoken to her in fifteen years. He does not like her. I say fine, but also, see if you can write in her voice, if you can empathize with her feelings as well.

He says, I don't know what she would say.

I say, Try to imagine how she feels.

He says, That would be my feelings, not hers.

I explain what empathy is and he says, Oh, I've done that hundreds of times and it does no good.

Afterwards, when I am with Marlis in her office she says, Wesley is so annoying, isn't he! And I say, Yes! Will Wesley ever take time to think about things instead of responding with a knee-jerk reaction? Then again, he was dangled in a basket from a winch when he was a little boy while his grandfather stood by laughing.

Preston tells us that he went to university. He talks about how Rumi could not read or write. I think that is apocryphal, but don't contradict him. Later I look this up and learn that Rumi was a scholar but Shams, the wandering dervish who became one of the most important people in Rumi's life, may have been illiterate.

Why should I be surprised that there is always something new to learn, especially when you think you are familiar with a subject?

WEDNESDAY, OCTOBER 15

Several of the men come late to the workshop. They were at the dog training sessions. They are happy to spend time with dogs, training them, petting them, feeding them.

This is one of the few programs at the correctional facility. Only a dozen inmates have helped train about seventy puppies for adoption since the launch of the WOOF program (Working On Our Future) began.

I learned that Justice Minister Landry, along with a dog trainer and an inmate, say the program is working. "Offenders have described their participation in the program as life-changing ... Staff at the facility tell us the program has helped reduce tension and has strengthened the relationship between staff and offenders."[49] The Justice Minister announces that the pilot program launched in December will be extended for a full year at the Central Nova Scotia Correctional Facility at a cost of $60,000.

Yet despite the small amount of money allotted for this program, there is opposition. The leader of the provincial Progressive Conservatives says the money spent on the program is misplaced. "It may be a good program, but you have to question the government's priorities when there are so many other pressing needs."

The Justice Minister says, "It costs $63,000 per year to house an offender. So if you make a difference in one person's life, that more than covers the cost."

One inmate, who came from the dog training sessions, says, Everybody who sees a dog, they don't think of anything else. They pick up the dog. They play with it. It's an easier time with the dog around.

Marlis isn't available when I come to give the workshop. She forgot there was a workshop today. Chris, another CO, agrees to come to the workshop. He is bored and shakes his foot during the session; his eyes glaze over when I read poems. But the inmates listen.

Kenny has been in the hospital recently. He is a heroin addict and has problems with his heart. But he is here this week and listening.

Last week they gave their notebooks to Marlis so the prose pieces they wrote could be photocopied for me, but she never returned their notebooks to them. I hand out loose paper for them to write on.

I give out the poem "Persimmons" by Li-Young Lee[50] and though I read a censored version which I typed up and which omits a graphic description of love-making, they still laugh when I read the lines about eating persimmons (*Chew the skin, suck it, and swallow*). I ask them to write about a teacher they liked or one they hated, as the poet did in the poem.

Paul writes about nuns who were mean-spirited and evil. I was the only Indian kid among all those white kids at school, he says. He tells us that when he asked if he could go back into the school to get his homework, the nun hit him hard with an umbrella. She hit with force too if she ever heard him speak Mi'kmaq.

Warren writes about how it was hard for him to learn because he was always defending his brothers and sisters. He describes the cruel nuns with their beady dark eyes.

WEDNESDAY, OCTOBER 22

Travis says, The sad thing is I was sick, nearly died of cancer, and here I am doing petty crime and spending years in prison. But I'm past that!

He writes, I'm grateful to be intelligent enough to learn from the experience of prison and to be a better person instead of a bitter person. He says he had stage four cancer, and he recovered. And then he was arrested for petty thievery. He says he has to change his ways. Then he says, So enough about me. Tell me about your week! How is Carole?

How could I not love Travis?

I say, Martha Stewart said there are worse things than prison, and all the men agree. I ask them to give me an example. Emery says, My daughter nearly died. That was worse than prison. She had a bowel obstruction but our local hospital did not diagnose it correctly. That hospital is terrible. She was transferred to the IWK in Halifax. Later I learned that had she spent one more day in that local hospital she would have died.

Warren says, It's jail here, not prison. When I ask what the difference is, he says prison has people patrolling with guns. Jail doesn't. I thank them for educating me.

WEDNESDAY, OCTOBER 29

Marlis does not want to sit in on this workshop. I don't think she is interested in poems; when I hand them out she usually reads the newspaper. She asks if I mind if Avery, the social work student, sits in during the next few workshops instead. Avery is interested in joining the workshop.

I give out the poem "Samurai Song" by Robert Pinsky[51] and ask the men to take one line from the poem and write about it. For instance, if they choose

> *When I had no father I made*
> *Care my father*

they can write about how taking care of themselves and others became important to them at some point in their lives, or less important to them, and why this happened, as well as what they mean by "taking care."

I remember one of my students at Dalhousie took the line,

> *When I had*
> *No lover I courted my sleep*

and followed it with the line,

> *And even sleep held out on me.*

I shared that response when I gave workshops with women in the prison and we laughed and marvelled at the student's creativity. I am not comfortable enough to share that line with the men's group.

Or, if they'd rather not do that assignment, they can write about someone who inspired them.

Preston has written about Lowell, who inspires him. Lowell let Preston rent a house in exchange for helping him stack wood. Lowell is an environmentalist and a philanthropist who lives modestly. He is in his nineties yet is still active, attending meetings with organizations that work to protect the environment. I tell Preston I too am inspired by Lowell.

I give them the poem "On the Amtrak from Boston to New York City" by Sherman Alexie.[52] In the poem a woman on the train asks the narrator if he has seen Walden Pond. The narrator is tired of hearing about Walden Pond, and about Don Henley saving it. We talk about Walden Pond and Thoreau, names that are not recognizable to the participants. But they know who Don Henley is. They have heard "Hotel California."

The poem ends with Alexie talking about what he will say when someone *from the enemy* thinks he is *one of their own*. The men and I discuss what we think Alexie means by *the enemy* and how history is often written by the victors who obscure what really happened.

Before they leave I read them "Don't Do That," a poem by Stephen Dunn[53] in which the Rottweilers give advice. At the end of the poem the narrator gets down on all fours with the dogs as they lick his face. He wants to mess up the party downstairs, act wild and eat all the hors d'oeuvres. But the dogs tell him not to do that. They tell him to calm down and assure him that after a while the people who are giving the party are sure to open the door and let the dogs out.

The Rottweilers promise him,

> *and everything*
> *you might have held against them is gone,*
> *and you're good friends again. Stay, they said.*

Warren says, The dogs are more human than the people in the poem.

I ask them to write a piece in which an animal appears and tells them something. I won't be here to listen to the piece, I say, but they can share it with each other.

Write something that surprises you, I say. Ask the animal to speak and listen to what the animal says.

This was my last session on the North Wing. After the men leave Avery says, You want the guys to speak and they won't and then you put a piece of paper in front of them and they are so open and share so much.

I tell Marlis I will go to the women's section next. Marlis says, I thought the women weren't into poetry last time you went.

Did I say that? The women were distracted and didn't believe they knew much, but each group of participants is different. And the women I met in the East Wing were unforgettable. I would like to invite any woman who is interested to take the next workshop.

Then Marlis surprises me. She wants to show a film she saw on television about teaching poetry in prison, and wants all the men who took the workshop to be there. She says she thought of the workshops I give when she saw the documentary. I am so glad she discovered this film. I have not seen it but am interested. I tell her it would be great if all the men could be there, but some men have appointments during this time, and some of the men are getting released. I suggest she just pick a day and show the film. Months later, when I see her in the corridor, she says she did show the film and the men liked it a lot. I did not know Marlis cared that much.

Avery tells me to come with her to the East Wing so we can arrange a time for the workshops for women. She speaks to a corrections officer there. I ask if I can come Wednesdays and the CO says abruptly, Wednesdays are no good. I tell her I teach Tuesdays and Thursdays and she says, Come Mondays. I say, I don't think Mondays will work and she says, Then don't come at all.

Okay, I'll come this Monday! I say.

The CO scowls and says, Now she is telling us she'll come in a few days! It's on you to organize this, Avery, she snaps.

Is there a lot to organize? I wonder. All we need is a room and women who are interested in writing. The pens and paper are in the supply cabinet.

Avery says she'll organize the workshop.

I don't remember who the CO was who snapped at us that day. But once we were on the East Wing, all the COs were supportive. Everyone has difficult days in the correctional facility, I remind myself.

Bail conditions too hard to meet[54]

People with financial and mental
health problems are not always able to meet
onerous bail conditions says

Nova Scotia Legal Aid
executive director. For youths and adults who have
not been convicted yet are in jail awaiting trial –

between 10 and 11 per cent are either
African Nova Scotians or Indigenous Peoples.
Yet they represent only about 2 and 4 per cent

of the population respectively.
"Very serious, violent offences
make up a very small proportion of people

who are charged at all
and certainly serving remand," Megan Longley says,
executive director of Nova Scotia Legal Aid.

Allegations of property and drug offences, as well as
breaching bail conditions –
that's why most people are in jail on remand.

If you're accused of bludgeoning to death
your multi-millionaire father
and your uncle pays a $50,000 surety

do you have to stay in prison,
on remand,
until your trial?

According to Statistics Canada[55]

In the last ten years.
the number of people awaiting trial while in
Nova Scotia has increased threefold.

The daily average increased from 112
to 328 people
between 2004 and 2015.

People who are remanded are presumed
innocent and have not been convicted
of any offence.

For 2014-2015, Nova Scotia
had the highest proportion of inmates
(68 per cent) who were in jail on remand in the
country.

Ten years earlier,
the figure for Nova Scotia
was 38 per cent.

CHAPTER EIGHT

MONDAY, NOVEMBER 3

Avery suggests we limit the workshop to four women. This turns out to be a good idea as the women are more open and able talk about what is deeply important to them when there are only a few people in the room. Avery made sure a room was available and that everyone had paper and pencils. The four women were Patricia, Lauren, who is a young Mi'kmaw woman, Amalia, and Julia, a woman in her late thirties who seems weighed down by difficulties.

I hand out the poem "Ithaka" by Constantine Cavafy.[56] Though Cavafy might be mistaken for a poet who lived in ancient times because of his unusual language and historical themes, he was born in the later half of the 1800s. He wrote "Ithaka," inspired by Odysseus's journey home, in 1911. Though Odysseus's goal in *The Odyssey* is to reach Ithaka, arriving is not the achievement; the journey is more significant than the destination. What travellers learn on their journey is what gives meaning to their lives. The poem ends,

Keep Ithaka always in your mind.
Arriving there is what you're destined for.

But don't hurry the journey at all.
Better if it lasts for years,
so you're old by the time you reach the island,
wealthy with all you've gained on the way,
not expecting Ithaka to make you rich.

Ithaka gave you the marvelous journey.
Without her you wouldn't have set out.
She has nothing left to give you now.

And if you find her poor, Ithaka won't have fooled you.
Wise as you will have become, so full of experience,
you'll have understood by then what these Ithakas mean.

I tell them that Cavafy, who is revered today, published little in his lifetime and was known by very few. In an essay about Cavafy, E.M. Forster wrote, "Such a writer can never be popular. He flies both too slowly and too high."[57]

I ask the women to write about their own Ithacas, the place they hope or hoped to arrive. What have they learned, this far, on their journey? I ask.

Lauren writes that even in jail she feels she has arrived because she is no longer running and hiding and feels calmer. She has written a spiritual piece full of patience and gratitude. Julia cries as Lauren reads it.

Later, when Julia reads what she wrote, about being on a beach in the Philippines, she cries again. She says she felt so alive in the Philippines, and open to new experiences. I say, It's good you are crying. It means you are in touch with sadness, and then the sadness can leave. I hope someone cries every week! I say this because I don't want her to be embarrassed. I don't tell her how sad I feel, and how helpless to reassure her that she will have many positive experiences. I hope this is true, but I don't want to offer platitudes when she is grieving.

Patricia writes that her cousin said she would look after Patricia's daughter while Patricia is in jail, but then her cousin disappeared and now her daughter is in foster care. Patricia doesn't know how or when she will see her again. She is anxious. Women who have young children and are in prison are so vulnerable, and given little support. Patricia's situation seems, to me, unbearable.

Next we read a poem by Kay Ryan, "On the Nature of Understanding."[58] The poem is about thinking you've made great progress taming something wild. It is a tall, thin poem with only three or four words on most lines, as if it were a snake about to attack. The poem, about thinking you've tamed a wild thing, ends,

> *So it's*
> *strange when it*
> *attacks: you thought*
> *you had a deal.*

Lauren says, That poem says a lot. Like being here in prison, thinking you've come to terms with it and then you get so frustrated and feel miserable and trapped.

Amalia, a woman in her twenties whose long, dyed, ash blonde hair is so light it looks white, says her dream is to have children and a husband to care for. I tell her I will bring in Sharon Olds' poem "Looking at Them Asleep." It is about love that burns in you with a consuming intensity when you first have children and they are dependent on your care. Maternal love, in my experience, is as intense, and lasts longer, than the initial intoxication of falling in love. The poem also speaks to me about the passion and intensity of writing poems.

MONDAY, NOVEMBER 10

Lauren, Patricia, Amalia, and Julia have arrived for their second session. Julia, who cried during the first session, says she has a twin boy and girl and they are very close. Then says she lost a child on Halloween. The baby died after trick or treating because of a hole in her lung. She lost another child who lived only a few moments after birth. The death of a child is one of the worst traumas anyone can endure. I wonder if she has received help for PTSD.

When I read Tom Pow's poem "Loving, Writing,"[59] I tell them the origin of the poem. Tom Pow travelled to South America when he was a young man with a folder of his poems that he was working on. When his backpack was stolen, he lost all his poems. He had not made copies – this was before computers – and he was in deep despair. Then he wrote "Loving, Writing," which was a comfort to him when he completed it. The poem ends,

> In loving, in writing, how can you
> hold onto a finished thing? Whether
> you lose it or put it beneath glass,
>
> it is the act itself you must cherish.
> For what's left when the moment has passed,
> the wind will carry. Despite you.

Lauren asks if this was about loving or writing. I tell her I think the poem is about both. We talk about the last line. You can control your actions, but not the response to your actions. We talk about the line, *In loving, in writing, how can you hold on to a finished thing?*

Lauren says she has a lot of experience letting go. She does not elaborate.

We also read "Sleep Chains," by Anne Carson.[60] Avery, the social work student, says she doesn't get this poem. But math is my thing, not English, she says. I tell her not to worry about understanding the poem, but to listen to the sounds and see if they are pleasing. Sometimes sounds alone convey a lot. We talk about what a cicatrice is – a scar, and how scars, and what caused them, can rattle us. The rhythm and the alliteration in the last two lines, as well as the anaphora, of "pity" "pity" and "ocean" "ocean," and the assonance in the words "ocean" and "go," evoke powerful emotion. At least for me they do.

> *Here we go mother on the shipless ocean.*
> *Pity us, pity the ocean, here we go.*

I ask the women to write a letter to the little girl each woman was. Write to this five- or six-year-old girl, I say. Remember what she liked, what games she played, which toys were her favourite. Tell her what you love about her, how beautiful she is, how funny, and kind. Perhaps that little girl was never told these things, and now you must tell her, because she has been short-changed.

Patricia does not think she can write this letter. I ask if she was unhappy when she was young. No, she says. Then she says she was depressed. I ask her to try to remember that girl and see if she can reach out to her.

Lauren begins immediately and writes several pages.

Julia is the first person to read her piece. She writes about games she played, how she could amuse herself playing alone for hours.

Amalia writes about a dog she loved, how this dog was her best friend, how she loves animals and taking care of animals. When she was a little girl, the dog would sleep beside her when she cried herself to sleep.

Patricia's voice is shaking as she reads. One of the things she wrote to her young self was: No one should have to see what you saw. I am sorry your mother could not care for you, and your father was always drunk.

I say, How powerful this piece is, Patricia. You're brave to go back to that place and comfort that little girl.

Lauren is eager to read, but we are going around the circle and it is Avery's turn to read next. Avery speaks about being a tomboy as a kid, and says to her young self, Don't let anyone decide what's right for you. Stay your own person.

Finally it is Lauren's turn. She starts reading and begins to cry when she speaks about her brothers and how they would pull her in the snow on a sled. She cries when she reads about wanting to be a doctor, and how hard she worked in school.

MONDAY, NOVEMBER 17

Julia, Amalia, Patricia, and Lauren are here today. I ask the women to write about someone they know who had a very hard time. Lauren reads her piece first about her cousin who has cystic fibrosis. She writes that he helped her when she was going through withdrawal from addiction. She had been putting poison into her healthy body, while her cousin was trying hard just to stay alive with a weakened body. He tells her often how much he loves her. He is always positive. She writes that when he did a prayer dance and kissed the grass, another cousin said he could feel the spirit tremble. We are all moved by her piece.

Julia says she thinks the piece she wrote is boring. I ask if she will read it anyway.

She reads about one Christmas when her mother bought presents and asked Julia to help wrap them. The clothes Julia wrapped were too small for her brother and the toys too childish for her but when she asked who they were for her mother told her to wait and see. Her mother knew it would be a difficult Christmas because their father had broken his back earlier that year and they didn't have money for presents, but that Christmas she had them all get in the truck with a turkey dinner. Julia thought, Oh, we are going to Granny's, but instead they stopped at a strange house. Her mother told the woman, who came to the door with her two children, that she knew it was a hard Christmas for her because the woman's husband had died and she was on her own with the children. Julia's mother hoped the woman didn't mind that her family brought some gifts and wanted to share Christmas supper with them. The woman burst into tears.

I am about to cry too. Wasn't that a moving story, I say. And you thought it was boring! But it is so well written. We are not always the best judge of our own work, I add.

I ask Julia how she feels about sending what she wrote to her mother. She says her mother and father have no contact with her. They don't trust her. She reads the obituaries to see if they are still alive. She is grateful they visit her children, who are with her mother-in-law. She says her parents don't even know if she is alive.

I say that if she sent the piece she wrote to them, with a note saying she is thinking of them, I imagine they would be happy. I certainly would be very glad to get a letter from a son or daughter of mine if I hadn't heard from them in a long time.

Julia says, My mother said I have to prove I am trustworthy. I do not ask her to explain.

I send Julia's story to the same newsletter that I sent Jonah's story and Julia's story is accepted for publication there as well. I ask Avery to get a bio from her and this is what Julia wrote:

```
Julia is a 37 year old woman raised
in Newfoundland. The eldest of two
children, and mother of three, which
includes twins. She has battled de-
pression and found herself serving
time for fraud. She enjoys writing
as she finds her emotions flow from
her body through the pen and out
onto the paper. She looks forward to
a positive future as a mother, sis-
ter and daughter.
```

I tell Julia I love what she wrote.

Patricia writes about her grandmother who is her "rock." Her grandmother's daughter was raped and murdered when the little girl was three. This was Patricia's mother's youngest sister and Patricia's mother was caring for her at the time. A cousin was the man who raped and murdered the little girl. Patricia does not go into details of how and when the little girl was killed, but she says that her mother always felt guilty that she had not been able to protect her little sister. Patricia's mother died at thirty-five, Patricia writes. All my grandmother had was me and my daughter Tara and now I robbed her of that, Patricia says. She hopes her grandmother will be successful in getting custody of Tara while she is in jail. I ask if she can forgive herself for being in jail rather than feeling guilty. I ask if feeling guilty ever helps anyone.

For her in-class assignment she writes about saying goodbye to her three-year-old daughter and then turning herself in to the authorities because that was the deal. Her daughter held onto her neck as if she knew she would not see her mother again. It was a very sad piece. Almost everyone in the group cries. I cry as well.

In class Lauren writes about her brother who died in a car accident when he was twenty-three. She was only nine. He'd had a fight with his parents, went out in the car angry, and died in an accident that night. Before he left the house he made her promise that she would go to university. She promised. He told her he loved her. This is another writing session where everyone cries as they listen to each other's stories.

I tell these women that they are all working so hard and I congratulate them. I ask if they have any subject they want to write for homework and Lauren suggests they write about mistakes they made and how even mistakes helped them learn things. A great idea, I say. I would never be so bold as to ask them to write about mistakes.

MONDAY, NOVEMBER 24

Avery, the social work student who usually comes to meet me at the entrance of the prison, is not here. The guards tell me I can go on through on my own. I wonder if I can find my way through the prison maze to the East Wing. But when I go through the first set of doors, Avery is there. She says she is in the middle of writing three papers but came today only because of the workshop. How I appreciate her energy and enthusiasm.

Again, Lauren, Patricia, Amalia, and Julia are in the workshop. Julia tells me that after my suggestion the other week she had her lawyer contact her parents.

She tells me what the lawyer said when he got in touch with her mother and it was this – her mother doesn't want anything to do with Julia. Her mother said she is better off without her. Julia caused her enough grief.

I am stunned. I'd told Julia I was sure her parents would be grateful if she reached out to them. All I can think of, to comfort her, is to quote Thich Nhat Hanh: *When another person makes you suffer, it is because he suffers deeply within himself, and his suffering is spilling over. He does not need punishment; he needs help.*

What do you think? I ask. I have been wrong about her mother and I don't know if any words I share will have meaning for her.

She says she will think about it. Then she says, Why don't you write about what you learned from us? That's your assignment.

How generous she is to include me as a participant in the workshop. I thank her and tell her I will do the assignment. I ask if I can write about what happened when she sent the story to her parents. She nods.

Patricia says she showed her grandmother the piece she wrote and her grandmother cried. Why are you crying, Patricia asked, and her grandmother said she was crying happy tears. She wanted Patricia to mail the piece to her.

Did you? I ask.

Not yet. I'll mail it in my Christmas card.

I ask the women to write about someone who is important to them.

Patricia writes about her grandmother again. How her grandmother would always help people in the area. When a crazy guy would come by and beg her for cigarettes, she'd always keep the guy away from Patricia, but she'd give him a pack of smokes. One day he was walking down the road with a rope in his hand. Her grandmother called out, Where you going with the rope?

To hang myself, he said.

Look, if I give you smokes and ten dollars, will you give me the rope?

And he did.

My grandmother says when I get out of prison I can come back and live with her without paying any rent and get a job and get myself together so I can get my daughter back, Patricia says.

Good plan, the social worker says. I ask where her grandmother lives and she says the name of the town.

Your grandmother should talk to my mother, Julia says.

I pass out quotes by Joseph Campbell and everyone reads a quote and talks about what they think it means.

I read, *The cave you fear to enter holds the treasure you seek.*

What cave do I fear to enter? I wonder out loud. Patricia says, Life. Avery asks her to explain.

I'm afraid of life. I'm afraid when I get out of here I won't be able to get custody of my daughter, Patricia says.

I tell her I believe that if she is determined, she will get her daughter back. Does she think she will be a good mother, I ask and she says, with conviction, Yes. Good, I say. I tell her I think that if she doubts herself, that will hold her back.

Amalia writes about how she was in a car accident and her face was bruised and she felt ugly, but her boyfriend told her she was beautiful and took good care of her. She is not with him now, he was abusive to her, but he was able to be kind during that difficult time.

Patricia says, I used to make mistakes more than once just to make sure they really were mistakes.

After the workshop Avery walks me out to the front lobby. I wonder out loud why Julia's mother won't have any contact with her.

There are two sides to this story, Avery says. Maybe she treated them badly too many times. Even if it's blood, sometimes you have to wash your hands of someone. I've seen too many kids manipulate their parents.

I nod and leave. But I can't help thinking that no matter what Julia did, she is still the one in jail reaching out to her parents. They are not in jail. Can't they show mercy?

TUESDAY, DECEMBER 2

Julia, Amalia, Lauren, and Patricia are here again today.

I give out the poem "Not Waving but Drowning" by Stevie Smith.[61] It ends,

> *I was much too far out all my life*
> *And not waving but drowning.*

When I ask what the poem is about Patricia says, About drowning.

Julia says, It's about pretending you're fine when you're not.

Oh wow. I missed that, Patricia says.

Julia says that for her entire life she felt she was pretending. Like when she got her sentence. The lawyer said her sentence would be light, probably a few months. But she got a twenty-month sentence. She realized then that she wasn't really fine with any of what was happening.

I ask the women to write about a time they pretended to feel a certain way, but felt quite differently.

Patricia says she doesn't know what to write.

Avery says she can give an example. On weekends she is a bouncer and that past weekend she had to tell one of the women at the bar to leave because the woman was very drunk. The woman started cursing, calling her a cunt, and said she wouldn't leave. Avery said, You're drunk. You can either leave peacefully or not. Then Avery said the woman called her a psycho dyke. Avery was so angry. She got the woman out of the bar, but then she had to go back and be friendly and relaxed and act like nothing was wrong, though, inside, she was seething.

I thank her for that example. I feel honoured that she trusts us all with this story.

Lauren reads a piece she wrote during the week about her grandmother who was taken to a residential school when she was five. It affected my whole family, Lauren writes, because my grandmother was raped and abused, and though she had seven children when she was an adult, she couldn't love them and my mother couldn't love me.

She talks about how her mother was not kind to her nor did she understand her. Lauren says all her brothers ended up addicts and in prison. My mother should have learned something by now about her children and how she raised them, Lauren says.

She wrote that when she was nineteen she moved in and took care of her grandmother, who was suffering from Alzheimer's. She described outbursts her grandmother would have and how she would calm her down. Lauren would go out briefly and her grandmother would lean out the window and yell, Lauren, back come here. Her grandmother once said to her, Lauren, you are the only one who loves me. After she reads her piece she says, You told me to be specific and I tried to be.

I tell her what she has written is wonderful. The details she included are vivid and help the reader empathize with her and her grandmother. I say the story is a unique and one that only she could have written.

After everyone has spoken, I give out the poem "At the Wellhead" by Seamus Heaney[62] about his blind neighbour. It has the line,

> *Being with her*
> *was intimate and helpful, like a cure*
> *you didn't even notice happening.*

For homework I ask the women to write about someone they knew who was *helpful, like a cure.*

MONDAY, DECEMBER 8

Lauren, Julia, and Amalia are here. Patricia didn't come. She was upset because she is being moved to another day room. Amalia says, They are moving her in with the crazies. I don't know what happened but gather someone complained about her.

They have all done the assignment. Julia says she never knows what to write about and thinks about the assignment all week and then finally sits down and writes.

And you always write something that is powerful, I say.

She reads her story about how similar she is to her father, how he too hides his feelings. As she reads she starts to cry. She describes how she and her father spent time repairing a car and when they finished and it was perfect her mother destroyed it. I can not tell from the story how her mother destroyed it, but Julia writes that she did so because she was jealous that Julia and her father were spending time together. Julia writes that she feels guilty that she left but her father is still there.

Amalia says she too thinks she doesn't know what to write about and all week she is anxious. Then she reads her piece about her mother who always made sure she was clean and well dressed. She still speaks to her every day on the phone. She also reads a piece she wrote about her dog, who is her best friend and her protector. I tell her it is good to hear that she and her mother are close.

Lauren reads a detailed piece about her father, how loving he was. He was the caregiver.

Lauren says she is getting out next week but is nervous. She will have to live with her mother, and be back in the same environment where she took drugs. She doesn't want to take drugs again or drink and will have to be strong. She will try to get a job and her own place as soon as she can.

Amalia says she is nervous about getting out as well, even a bit depressed. I ask Amalia if she will be living with her mother. She says no, she is lucky, she is moving back with her boyfriend. Not the boyfriend who abused her – a new boyfriend she has been with for a year. They have decided to have a baby as soon as they can. She knows she can't drink or do drugs. All her friends do drugs and she doesn't think it's her place to tell them not to. Her boyfriend won't do drugs around her or drink but when he goes out with his friends she wants him to feel he can do what he wants. Her parents judge her friends but she doesn't feel it's right to judge them.

Avery tells her that she may think she has a lot in common with these friends, but if they are all doing drugs and she isn't she'll find they don't have much in common and she will drift away from them. I would be hesitant to say this because I am their parents' generation and the young women may feel I am out of touch. But Avery is close to their age; I think her words will have impact.

These are his friends, Amalia says, and she accepts his friends. She says she would do anything for them. She still loves her old boyfriend who was abusive, and would do anything for him as well. She says his parents still contact her and she loves them too. Her new boyfriend knows this.

Lauren says she feels bad for Amalia because if Amalia loved herself she wouldn't say that about a man who abused her.

Julia, who sent the Christmas story she wrote to her parents, at my suggestion, and was told they want nothing to do with her, and who will be in prison until next November, doesn't say anything.

I hand out the poem "Power" by Adrienne Rich.[63] Rich, writing about Marie Curie, ends the poem with the line, *her wounds came from the same source as her power.*

This is literally true of Marie Curie, who suffered from radiation sickness because of the years she spent purifying radium. Adrienne Rich writes that Marie Curie denied what had given her cataracts and caused her skin to crack. The poem ends,

She died a famous woman denying
her wounds
denying
her wounds came from the same source as her power.

But this dual source is true of all of us, if we examine our strengths and how we developed them, I say. If we are willing to explore why we feel hurt, and how we react because of the pain, we begin to understand ourselves and this understanding is our power.

Lauren says it is hard for her when people judge her for being in prison, and she would be humiliated if a university turns her down because she has been in prison. I say she can claim her experience and she can use it to her advantage, she can wear it like a badge of honour. Few others in the university will know anything about being incarcerated and she can share what she has learned firsthand.

Avery doesn't say anything during the workshop, but later when we are alone she says to me, Inmates need to be careful who they tell about being in prison because although *Carole* says they could use it as a badge of honour, most people will judge them harshly so it is better not to mention it unless they have to. I agree. I didn't choose my words wisely. In fact, I don't think of prison as a badge of honour, but as an experience that will give inmates a perspective that non-inmates will not have. I thank Avery for, once again, being honest with me.

MONDAY, DECEMBER 15

This Monday is the last day of the seven-week writing workshop on the East Wing. The first time I gave a workshop here the women who participated had no confidence. These women also lack confidence but they are open to talking about their experiences. A small workshop has given participants this opportunity.

These women work hard and share so much.

The last day I pass out the following quotes from Rumi and each of us reads a quote and speaks about it. We continue reading as we go around the circle until we read all the quotes:

Your task is not to seek for love, but merely to seek and find all the barriers within yourself that you have built against it.

What you seek is seeking you.

If you are irritated by every rub, how will your mirror be polished?

Don't grieve. Anything you lose comes round in another form.

You were born with wings, why prefer to crawl through life?

After the Rumi quotes, participants read the pieces they wrote during the week. Julia cries as she reads what she wrote about her children. Most of the women in prison are young, have had children, and many are not sure if they will regain custody or when they will see their children again.

At the end of the session I read a poem of mine, "Kimberly Rogers," from *Church of the Exquisite Panic: The Ophelia Poems*,[64] about a woman arrested for welfare fraud. Julia says, That's why I am here, for welfare fraud. I shudder. Julia and I have more in common than she knows.

When I left my first husband, I had two children under the age of three. I knew I would not have the energy to care for them and work full-time, even if I were lucky enough to get a full-time job. I went on welfare. I was grateful for the opportunity to stay home with my sons.

In Canada, if you get money from welfare and don't declare that you are also attending university or that your ex-husband helps with bills, or that you have earned money giving a workshop, then you are breaking the law. But the money welfare provides is not enough to pay rent and buy food and diapers, much less provide for a few pleasures, like going out occasionally and paying for a babysitter.

I struggled every month to pay bills. And then I was invited to give a workshop at the Labrador Creative Arts Festival for a week. A friend took care of my sons during that time, and I flew to Labrador; the festival paid for the ticket. It was an intense and inspiring week working with children and adults, giving readings, meeting other writers as well as artists and musicians, seeing plays put on by students. I was flown to Nain to give a workshop as well. And I earned money. I think I earned about $500 for the week's work, a substantial sum for me at the time.

Did I report it? Yes, but I said much of it went to the babysitter, which was not true. I did not have to pay my friends who watched my children. I was nervous about lying, but the money I earned would have been deducted from the money I received from welfare that month. So I too committed welfare fraud.

Later, I say to Avery that it is such a shame Julia is in jail for welfare fraud. Avery says, We don't know the whole story.

I do not tell her about my history, but I point out that women accused of this crime are not jetting off to Paris for the weekend; they are barely able to pay their bills. If these women in the workshop had been wealthy, they would not be on welfare. We attack the most vulnerable.

She reluctantly agrees. But she is right as well. I don't know the whole story.

When I leave, the women say that there will be no more programs on their unit.

In February the student who started the literary journal accepts Lauren's piece about her grandmother for publication. I write to Lauren to let her know, as she gave me her email address. This is her response:

```
Wow! What great news!
     I am submitting one of my
writings into this aboriginal contest
and I was just thinking last night
about the piece I wrote in prison
that the journal might publish but I
haven't heard back from them. This
is so exciting. Of course she has my
permission. I will write a bio and
attach it when I complete it. Thanks
for such a great opportunity Carole.
     I am doing great as well. I'm
expecting my first child.
     - Lauren
```

From the Annual Report, 2014-2015, Office of the Correctional Investigator[65]

Between 2005 and 2015, the Indigenous inmate population grew by 50% compared to an overall offender growth rate of 10%.

First Nations, Inuit and Métis inmates now represent just over 25% of the in-custody population despite comprising just 4.3% of the Canadian population.

Aboriginal inmates are more likely to be classified as maximum security,

spend more time in segregation

and serve more of their sentence behind bars compared to non-Aboriginal inmates.

Indigenous women make up less than 5 per cent of the population. They account for 38 per cent of women in prison.[66]

One Woman's Story[67]

"… At 37, [Amanda Lepine] the Métis woman from Manitoba says she's spent most of her life in prisons, starting when she was just 12.

"… She's currently serving eight-and-a-half years for her role in an armed robbery in Winnipeg in 2015. In a Winnipeg Police Service news release about the incident, police state that no injuries were reported and that cash and cigarettes were stolen from the store.

"… She talks about the sexual abuse she endured starting at the age of three, the substance abuse and chaos in her home, her experiences in the child welfare system and being thrown in the Winnipeg youth detention centre at 12.

"… 'I wouldn't call myself a victim,' she said. 'I think people just made bad choices for me and that's what happens in the system. You lose that control, you can't make choices for yourself and it sucks because you have all these people thinking they know what's best for you when they don't. When they're actually making your life worse.'

"… Being sent to an adult women's prison at 14 was probably the worst of her experiences with the justice system.

… "She says she first got involved with the youth justice system for running away from a foster home and says the child welfare system grew increasingly fed up with her behaviour, which at times involved thefts and other property crimes.

"When she was 14, she said, she was 'raised' to the adult prison and kept there for nearly five years.

"'I stayed in there until two weeks before my 19th birthday and yeah, I didn't see anybody. I didn't see my family. [Child and Family Services] didn't even come see me. And when they released me it was just, drop me off at the main mall and good luck with your life. Like, thanks.'"

Courage

I listen to a *Fresh Air* podcast about the film *Tower*,[68] an account of the mass shootings from a tower at the University of Texas when a sniper took the lives of sixteen people in the summer of 1966. Keith Maitland, the filmmaker, describes an incident he heard that made him want to make the film.

Claire Wilson, a pregnant woman and a freshman at the university, and her boyfriend, Tom Eckman, were walking across campus to put a nickel in the meter when Claire was shot by a gunman in the Tower. She lay bleeding on the hot cement in the burning sun, in the line of fire. Tom, the second person shot, died instantly.

In the film, made fifty years later, Claire describes how she looked up at the sky, which was "so blue," and thought, "I guess this is it."

But a young female student, Rita Murphey, ran to the woman and asked, "How can I help?" The wounded woman told her to leave, told her she was in danger. But she didn't leave. She crouched by the woman's feet, and talked to her. She told her she was going to be okay. She asked her questions about her life. She kept talking to make sure the woman remained conscious.

It was this woman who risked her life, Rita Murphey, who inspired Maitland to make the film. In an interview he talks about what it means to be heroic. "It's a woman lying down, offering compassion, and it is so deeply human. It is just about the bravest thing I ever heard."

Courage. How does one manifest courage in the world?

CHAPTER NINE

WEDNESDAY, JANUARY 14, 2015

My first thought, when I come to the workshop, is, Why only white men in this group? I wonder if the men are being segregated now.

I have been giving writing workshops for inmates at the Correctional Facility for a year and this is the first time there is no one of colour participating. Prisoners remanded here are waiting to be sentenced, some for minor offences, others for violent crimes – murder, rape. I rarely know what the inmates are accused of. I don't want to know. I don't want my impressions filtered through the lens of crimes they are accused of.

These men – Finn, Dennis, Joe, Karl, and Emerson – are from the West Wing. The corrections officer, Marlis, says no one else wanted to come to the workshop today. Sorry, she says.

Later I get this email from Shiloh, who has a poetry program on a local radio station where prisoners call in and read their poems on the air. She has a great rapport with the inmates who call. Shiloh writes,

> The Burnside guys want you to
> know that they all wanted to take
> the poetry course but they were

```
told only 5 can come. At least 10
other guys want to! I don't know
if that's a jail thing or what,
but they were hoping more of them
could take it or wondering if
there would be another one.
```

It seems that Marlis only let the men know about the workshop yesterday. I'll have to sort this out later.

Marlis looks relieved she does not have sit in on the workshop today. Instead, Avery and another social work student, Sebastian, join me.

In her next email, Shiloh writes,

```
Aw, my guys are on the West! I'll
pass the info to them so they
know. You're lucky, they're
sweethearts.
```

When a friend hears that these men, who may or may not be found guilty of committing violent crimes, are called "sweethearts," she wonders if crimes are being ignored in the attempt to offer rehabilitation through poetry. I understand this response. But Shiloh cares deeply about these men and dedicates much of her time to encourage them. I too, like Shiloh, feel lucky to work with the participants on the West Wing, and with other prisoners, many of whom are kind and enthusiastic. Their appreciation is deep and it is heartening to see how moved they are when they are honoured for the stories they share. Some students take for granted their inclusion in a class and their right to be heard. Not these men.

Today, instead of a complete poem I hand out excerpts by the thirteenth-century Sufi poet Rumi[69] and everyone reads one quote.

When you do things from your soul, you feel a river

moving in you, a joy gets a strong response. Karl says he knows exactly what Rumi means. He feels that river of joy.

Several of the men talk about the following Rumi quote: *Ignore those who make you fearful and sad, that degrade you back towards disease and death.*

I say, Okay, write about those who make you fearful, or those who help you get in touch with the *river of joy*.

Joe, who is from Cape Breton and missing a front tooth, says he does not know what to write.

Emerson says, Write about your brother or sister.

Joe says, Can I go back now? I'm feeling stressed.

But there is no guard to take him back. The room used for the workshop is locked, as is every room here.

Emerson says, Write about your first girlfriend, write about friends, write about anything. You're here now.

I suggest he write about a beautiful place he's enjoyed.

I've been in jail since I was twelve. I don't remember a beautiful place, Joe says.

Finn also says he was on his own since he was eleven.

Dennis writes how he was taken away from his family because they were abusive. He does not go into details but later says his father was an alcoholic and his mother a gambler. A family in Cape Breton took him in. They bought him new clothes and they treated him the same as they treated their own children. They were so good to him. He thinks about them often and about maybe getting in touch with them again but he hasn't. I ask how long he stayed with the family.

Four months, he says.

A period of four months that took place decades ago, and this is his most positive memory.

Karl writes that his mother's best friend had a husband everyone thought was great. Karl said he won't even go into the things this man did to him from when he was eight until he was eleven, it was so bad. But when he finally told on the man, and the man was going to be tried, Karl's mother asked for leniency. It seems her best friend had berated her saying, How can you let my husband go to jail? Karl says he felt so bad that his mother sided with her friend and not with him.

I admire how open Karl is, the opposite of self-pitying. There are no psychologists, no therapy, no counselling in this prison to help inmates heal. How can a six-week writing workshop help?

Emerson writes about hitchhiking with his girlfriend, having no money, no place to stay, and how a cleaning woman in northern Ontario gave them money to buy train tickets back East. He has never forgotten how kind the cleaning lady was.

While the other men write, Joe shakes his foot, stares at the paper, and at the inmates in the room. He listens as the men read what they wrote. As they file out to go back to their cells, I thank them each and shake their hands. Thank you, Dennis responds when I thank him. Thanks, Emerson says, shaking my hand. Joe says, I'll write something next week. He doesn't come back the following week, but at that moment he wants to.

WEDNESDAY, JANUARY 21

Karl seems to be nodding off during the workshop today. I ask if he is high. The other men laugh. Karl tells me he is on methadone, which is making him sleepy. I thank him for letting me know. I say that during the last workshop he was so present, so alert.

I ask the men to write a letter to the ten-year-old boy each was. Tell him what you remember about that little boy and describe what he liked, what games he played, what his favourite food was, what a sweetheart he was. Give details. Finn refuses to write the assignment. Going back to his childhood is too painful, he says. I hand out another poem, "Beauty" by Tony Hoagland.[70] It is about a middle-aged woman who has been ill and realizes she will never be beautiful again. But she tosses her head and shakes her beautiful curls, as if she were throwing out something she'd carried for a long time

> *but had no use for anymore,*
> *now that it had no use for her.*
> *That, too, was beautiful.*

I tell them the alternative assignment is to write about something that might not appear beautiful to an outside observer, but, to them, has beauty. They can title their piece "That too was beautiful."

Finn writes about growing up in Halifax in a public housing residential area. His was one of the few white families in a predominantly Black community and he was picked on often but after a while, if you followed the rules, things were fine. What were the rules? Everyone seemed to have the same thing in mind – look out for your neighbours and don't walk on their lawn. He writes that life at home was terrible but when he walked outside it was totally different.

"Strangers would let me swim in their pools, play basketball and invite me to their BBQs." He was welcome as part of the community. It may have looked like a rough neighbourhood but people looked out for each other, he writes, and that too was beautiful.

Jackson writes about his sister who was dying of cancer but was still drinking. He'd buy her liquor and when her husband came home she'd say the empty bottles were Jackson's and he'd take the blame. His other sisters attacked this sister, but he defended her. When she was hospitalized she said she just wanted to see her children and grandchildren before she died, so her husband brought her home. Jackson was there at the last dinner. And she never looked better, he said. She was only thirty-eight when she died.

Evan talks about what a high percentage of Black men there are in prison and that once you are a convict no one wants to hire you. And you can't lie because the employers find out. I tell him I agree with everything he says. But people do change their lives. I tell him there is no one like him, who has his experiences. And because of his experiences, he can be instrumental in helping others.

He nods. He says, Yeah. Then he asks if I think my giving workshops will be helpful. I say he can answer that better than I can. But I tell him that I believe any time anyone thinks carefully about a situation and writes in detail about what happened, it helps him or her think more clearly. I say I have faith that thinking more clearly helps people act with more clarity. Evan doesn't say anything. He just looks at me. He is nervous about getting out and what his life will be like out of prison. I can understand his fear.

At the end of the class Karl asks if he can talk to me. He says he was abused by a corrections officer and he wants to write the story. But who would publish it? he wants to know. I tell him to write it, not to worry about who will publish it. I say we'll talk about that after he writes it.

Later Avery says I embarrassed Karl when I asked if he was high. She politely suggests I could have talked to him in private. He was quieter in the workshop today than he was last week. Did the question I asked the previous week make him self-conscious today? I feel bad that I might have hurt Karl.

I get an email from Shiloh. She tells me about her friend who is in jail. She writes,

```
Oliver is in the hole right now at
Springhill. He didn't do anything,
only he's placed in a max so until
they transport them they put them in
solitary. He only gets calls twice
a week and other than that no human
contact. Last call he told me he's
talking and laughing to himself in
his cell and he hasn't been out for
10 days straight. It's just heart-
breaking, we all cry all the time.
Best, Shiloh
```

Shiloh writes,

```
I heard the guys enjoyed the work-
shop a lot. Evan called me to read
me his work. He seemed very pleased
and proud. He said, She has a thing
with things being beautiful!
```

DEATH OF CLAYTON CROMWELL[71]

A CBC News report from October 14, 2018, has the headline "Intercom found to have been intentionally disabled in Burnside jail death," followed by, "No response to emergency button in Clayton Cromwell overdose, report says."

"... a cellmate found ... Clayton Cromwell of Halifax unconscious on April 7, 2014, and yelled at other inmates with an intercom in their cell to press the 'red button.'

"But there was no response for 10 or 15 minutes, inmates said, and they had to start kicking doors and yelling to get attention of officers at the Central Nova Scotia Correctional Facility located in Dartmouth, N.S.

"... the intercom had been cut some time earlier, in contravention of provincial rules.

"'They used to have intercoms in there,' a captain is described as telling the corrections investigator. 'They were a nuisance for the most part.'"

An autopsy report showed Cromwell died of a combination of methadone and the anti-depressant benzodiazepine.

Cromwell, who was Black as are 10 percent of the population in federal prison, though Black Canadians are only 3 percent of the general population, was in the jail awaiting a hearing on an alleged charge of violating probation in a case of trafficking marijuana.

"He was repeatedly described by inmates as a 'good kid,' who'd been in the unit for a short period of time."

He was twenty-three.

* * *

At home, listening to CBC News, I learn new rules have been put in place because of this death.

Some of the inmates in my workshops are on methadone, which is given to prisoners addicted to heroin or other opioids. Though doctors administer opioids for physical pain, emotional anguish can drive inmates to seek the same numbing relief. The news item says that Cromwell had not been in the methadone program. "It's impossible for them to know exactly what happened that night, which is unfortunate because I think it speaks to the overcrowding, the understaffing and the lack of security that exists in that prison," Devin Maxwell, lawyer for the Cromwell family, said.[72]

There was a young man in one of my writing workshops at the prison whose last name was Cromwell. I forget his first name, and wonder if the man who died was in my workshop. I remember asking that young man if he knew about the history of Thomas Cromwell, minister to King Henry VIII, who helped annul the king's first marriage so he could marry Anne Boleyn. I said I'd recently read a very good novel, *Wolf Hall*, by Hilary Mantel, which she'd written from Cromwell's point of view.

When I look up the article in the paper, I see that the inmate who had died looks so young. Of course he would. He was twenty-three.

No, this man was not in my workshop. But he easily could have been.

There may have been new rules put in place and changes made in the way methadone is monitored because of Clayton Cromwell's death. But there have been no changes in the overcrowding and understaffing in the prison.

TUESDAY, JANUARY 27

Emerson, Will, and Jackson are here. It's cold outside, but in this room it's hot and the men are sweating in their short-sleeve T-shirts. I must remember to wear layers next week so I can take off my sweater.

I hand out a poem by Rainer Maria Rilke from his collection *The Book of Hours*.[73] The poem, "The Hour is Turning," ends,

> *My looking ripens things*
> *and they come toward me, to meet and be met.*

I say the more we look carefully at the world we live in, the more it reveals. I ask the men to write about someone they hate but for whom they can also feel compassion.

Emerson says he can't write about someone he hates, yet feels sorry for. I haven't gotten there yet, he says.

A conversation develops about bullies and I suggest the men write about someone they know who was bullied, or write about a time they were bullied or were bullies themselves.

Emerson says he doesn't think he should write about that because his case is coming to trial and it might look bad for his character development if he writes about his dark past. He says that his younger brother was bullied and someone smashed his brother's head. He ran after the guy and teachers had to hold him back because he had a temper and if he'd found the guy he might have killed him. I ask why he had an uncontrollable temper at such a young age and he says because he was bullied by other kids. I ask if he was

bullied at home by his parents and he says he is not go-
ing to get into that.

Sebastian, the social work student, agrees that it is
best he avoid this subject.

But it would be good to explore the subject at
some time, I say. Emerson agrees, and says he would
like to talk about it with a counsellor. Do the inmates
ever get to talk to a therapist? Inmates I've met say there
is a psychiatrist who prescribes drugs, but no therapist
to talk with.

For the homework assignment I give out the poem
by Martín Espada, "When Leather is a Whip."[74]

The men relate to this poem. We talk about want-
ing to protect people we love from bad memories and
future pain. For homework I ask the men to write about
someone they feel tenderly about, their mother or father
or brother, sister, friend, girlfriend, wife.

Emerson says there is no one he can write about.

I ask, There is no one you feel tenderly towards,
and who you know feels protective toward you? No one
who *has your back*, as they say. He says, No.

Sebastian asks Emerson if he can write about his
girlfriend. Emerson says he'd rather not. I say that it is
sad there was no one who looked out for him and tried
to protect and help him. He is quiet and looks absorbed
in his thoughts.

Then I hand out the poem "A Story"[75] by Czeslaw
Milosz. I hope this poem is more successful than his
poem "Dedication," which I'd printed for the women
on the East Wing. Before I can suggest an assignment,
Jackson says he doesn't understand what is happening
in the poem. We go over the narrative: a grizzly bear is
so malicious it batters the door of a cabin in the woods

and breaks the window with its paw. Later the narrator discovers the cause of the bear's uncharacteristic violence – the animal has an abscess in its tooth. It suffers

> *An ache without comprehensible reason*
> *Which often drives us to senseless action*
> *And gives us blind courage.*

I ask if the men can write about someone who was driven to senseless action. It can be themselves, or someone they know or knew. Can they write the details so we are able to see this person, as we see the bear in "A Story"? I understand this is a challenging assignment.

Emerson exclaims, That's what we were just talking about.

I'm silent. I am not quite sure what he means.

After a long pause he says, Having no one I could count on. That was the ache.

Unsaid, but echoing in the silence:

> *An ache without comprehensible reason*
> *Which often drives us to senseless action.*

I don't yet know the crime Emerson is charged with and to which he will later plead guilty.

* * *

Several faculty in the creative writing program are giving a reading at the university where I teach. Shiloh, a colleague at the university, and I are two of the six readers. Though I don't think Shiloh has met the men in my workshop, she communicates with them through the radio show she hosts and knows who they are; many have read their poems on her show. Right before we go to the podium she says something that makes me feel I am holding a bomb about to explode.

A few months ago the papers had a story about a woman living in the community who was reported missing. Her family and friends were frantic and they, as well as people in the community, were searching for her. Photos of this woman, in her twenties with her beautiful smile, were printed in the paper. She was doing important work. Everyone who read about her held their breath, hoping she was alive.

The papers stated that she had struggled with addictions in the past but had turned things around.

A few weeks after she went missing her body was found and two people were arrested.

This is a story of a woman who worked so hard to understand and change her life and help others change theirs, but was unable to escape brutality. I think, in a world where exploitation is prevalent, brutality is prevalent as well.

The question Shiloh asks is what do I think of Emerson. I wonder why she asks about this pale, quiet guy. This is the young man who wrote about going into the woods and seeing caterpillars that hung from trees by threads and how he'd spend hours staring at them, when I asked the men to write about a place that was special to them. This was the man who read the line, *An ache without comprehensible reason* and made the connection that his ache was having no one who cared about him.

Why do you ask about Emerson?

He's accused of killing ... and then Shiloh says the name of the woman people frantically searched for and whose body was discovered some days later.

How could Emerson have murdered her? When I'd first read the articles and heard the news, I saw the murderer as a monster, a crazed psychopath. But Emerson?

At the last workshop Emerson said that Karl helped him a lot. He listens to me; he exercises with me, Emerson says. Emerson appreciates any kindness shown to him. He seems nervous, a low-drip anxiety beneath his calm, though he laughs fully when someone makes a joke. He's twenty-five, the age of my younger son.

I ask my husband how Emerson could have done this. And Bill says, Anyone can cross the line if, if … There are so many ifs.

How will the family of the murdered woman endure their grief?

Yet only someone who has never known inmates could dismiss them by saying they are evil.

Someone I tell says, He was probably high. People do horrible and brutal things when they are drunk or high. So he murdered someone.

But I can never say, So he murdered someone.

Someone says, It's better if you don't know what the prisoners have done.

Better not to seek out this information, perhaps. But I read newspapers, listen to the news. It's inevitable I'll find out some of the crimes committed. But Emerson? This murdered woman? It's incomprehensible.

How do I treat him? I ask my husband. Anyone who has read about this woman can't help but feel robbed and outraged by her murder.

Treat him like you'd want your own son to be treated, Bill says.

From the little I've learned about Emerson, I know

that even as a little boy he was so furious his teachers had to hold him back, *or he would have killed the bully*. It sounds like his whole life contributed to who he became, a bomb about to go off. No one intervened to help him, though there were signs he needed help. And then there is his revelation that surprises even him, after he reads the Milosz poem about a crazed bear.

If I'd known at the first workshop that he was accused of killing this woman, I would have seen him differently. At the last workshop he said, I don't know if you read the papers. The reporter described me as walking like a fighter, but I was just trying to stand up straight.

At the time I didn't know why he was in court. I didn't look up the article. But now I do. The article that offended Emerson talks about his aggressive walk, and implies that his nose looks like it was broken, most likely in a fight.

Bryan Stevenson, an author as well as an attorney who fights for the wrongfully accused on death row in the American South, says, "Each of us is more than the worst thing we've ever done ... Even if you kill someone, you're not just a killer." He says, in one of his talks, "When you get close to inequality you will get broken. Because I am broken I can't live in a world where other broken people are being crushed ... We have demonized people and defined them by their worst acts. None of us wants to be defined that way."

Other prisoners know why Emerson is there, and they are able to befriend him, even if they are in jail for infractions that have not caused harm to anyone else.

They know a lot I don't know.

After one of the initial workshops with this group

on the West Wing, when I said I feel bad for these men, the corrections officer just nodded. She didn't seem sympathetic and I criticized her silently for being hard-hearted. But she knew why Emerson was there and didn't tell me; this was generous of her.

FEBRUARY 4

Dennis, Finn, Emerson, Jackson, Karl are here.

Evan is not well and does not attend.

Dennis, a young man, joins the group. The tattoo on his neck is comprised of the letters that spell SURVIVOR.

I ask what the letters on Jackson's knuckles are. He is embarrassed and says, You don't want to know. The others say, Tell her, she would probably appreciate it. He shows me one hand, letters on his fingers but not his thumb, and the fingers on the other hand as well. Each hand makes no sense, he says. But when he clasps his hands together the letters spell "Let's fuck."

Karl says his chest and back are covered with tattoos. He wishes he could remove 90 percent of them. On his neck is the name of his middle son, and the boy's birth date. On his arm, the initials of his other son. They look like twins, he says. They were born a few months apart, from different mothers.

He says that he has been in jail for twelve years, most of his adult life, and when the guards see his tattoos they think he is involved with a gang and they put him in lockdown. All these guys have been in lockdown. Karl tells me he was in lockdown for two years and nine months. How is that possible? How does someone remain sane during that isolation?

I hand out the poem, "Call Me by My True Names"[76] as well as quotes from several writers about compassion. I ask the men to each read a quote aloud and we go around the room. When we get to Finn he reads, *Compassion is the antitoxin of the soul: where there is compassion even the most poisonous impulses remain relatively harmless,* a quote by Eric Hoffer.

Finn says, You're bringing this in for us, and we can be compassionate, but in here, it's like putting tigers in a small cage and saying, Be nice to each other.

A powerful metaphor that makes me pause. Am I too naïve? Are such quotes ineffective? I have just learned what Emerson is accused of and am aware how little I know about these men. I don't know what they have done or what has been done to them, before and during incarceration.

I tell them Thich Nhat Hanh wrote "Call Me by My True Names" when he'd learned that a twelve-year-old girl had thrown herself into the sea after a pirate had boarded a boat carrying Vietnamese refugees and raped her. Thich Nhat Hanh could not sleep or eat after hearing this. He meditated throughout the night. When he wrote his poem, it was to remind himself that had he lived the life of the pirate, he might have done what this pirate did.

I ask the men if they can think of someone they are angry with, and write in this person's voice and from this person's perspective.

It is a difficult exercise. The men don't think they can do it. Perhaps I shouldn't have suggested it.

I ask them, instead, to write about a good deed they did.

Karl writes about a fight on the range. I learn that

range is another word for cell block or section where inmates are housed. Karl says he can't go into the details because then he will be considered a snitch. He said a guy got punched and was bleeding. Karl got his only towel, wet it, and bathed the wound. Another guy helped Karl bandage the wound. When the guards came in it was Karl who was put in solitary confinement, even though the guy who was beaten explained that Karl was helping him.

The men start complaining about how the guards just want to see them fight each other. Finn says that even though he hated the guy who was beaten up, he helped bandage the wound. Because it was the right thing to do.

So you show compassion under very difficult circumstances, and you know it is the right thing to do, even though you were punished for it, I say.

Dennis, the new guy, will not read what he's written, though all the men encourage him.

At the end of the workshop Karl says he would like to work with addicts, or troubled youth, to help them. If I could even help one person, it would be worth it, he says. What courses do I take? he asks. I tell him I don't know but I'll see what I can find out.

Career College, Finn says.

The social work student says no, you can't become a counsellor if you have a criminal record.

There are lots of ways to counsel and help people, I say.

Karl says, Yes, I could volunteer.

Not only volunteer, I say. There are organizations that work with people who are addicts. There are many ways to do what you want. Don't think that you can't do something just because you've been in prison. You've had experiences that no one else has had and with those experiences, you have understanding.

Finn says, How come you're so positive?

I say, I truly believe this. But I am touched because I think he understands that I believe in him and the other men in the workshop.

Later, we are waiting for the guards to come and open the door and lead the men back. The workshop has gone twenty minutes overtime. I say, Anyone know a good song? Can anyone sing something by Al Green?

Finn says, That's my grandmother's favourite singer. Me and your grandmother! I say.

Karl says, I like the song "Cat's Cradle," by the Harry Chapin guy. I never knew my father for the first eighteen years of my life and that song used to make me cry. Then I met him and lived with him and now I wish I hadn't. He'd get some dope and tell me to go out in the streets and sell it, or steal things.

After the workshop the social work student says, I have a lot of sympathy for Karl.

Impossible not to feel compassion and love for Karl.

WEDNESDAY, FEBRUARY 11

Finn was transferred to another jail. The guys say they won't miss him. Emerson, Karl, and Jackson are here.

Last week I asked them to list five things they are grateful for and Emerson is the first to share his list. He writes that he is grateful for

1. Being alive.

Yes, so am I, I say. What is unspoken is that some of the men here have deprived others of their lives.

2. The friends he has.

3. The relationship he has with his father, though he has had to get over hating his father.

4. He is grateful for books.

5. He is grateful for food.

Karl asks the corrections officer if she would mind getting him a glass of water. He is on medication and his mouth is dry. Marlis says she'll see what she can do. She leaves but does not come back and after a while Emerson gives Karl his apple juice. I am trying to be compassionate, Emerson says sincerely.

I ask them to write about a teacher who was very kind to them or a teacher who was cruel. Karl starts writing but says he has a lot to write about and can he finish during the week. When it is time for the men to share what they've written, he reads an older assignment that he did not get to read before, because he had to miss an earlier session.

He writes about how his stepfather Nigel used to take him to the dump on Saturdays, and they would watch bears open garbage bags as if the animals were kids opening Christmas presents. He always thought of Nigel as his real father even though he knew that was impossible because Nigel was Black and Karl has pale white skin. They'd sit on the hill by the dump, which was an illegal dump, and drink French onion soup. When I ask who made the soup Karl says his stepfather, who was from Jamaica and was a great cook.

I tell him how moved I am by his piece and what a tribute it is to his stepfather. When love is strong, any activity, even going to the dump, is special.

Karl says he didn't know his father's surname until he got his birth certificate. He ordered it and when it came he thought, What the hell. He asked his mother, Who is my father?

It took me a long time to stop hating my father, Emerson says, after Karl has spoken.

At the final workshop I tell the men how much I appreciated meeting them and hearing their stories. It was so generous of them to share so much, I say.

I know I will think about them all, especially Karl, who is so open and vulnerable.

Thank you, I say, when I shake Emerson's hand after our last session.

Thank *you*, he responds. Those two words will have to carry me a long time, where there are no answers and where so many questions are not even considered worthy of being asked.

Living while Black

"Though the white liberal imagination likes to feel temporarily bad about black suffering, there really is no mode of empathy that can replicate the daily strain of knowing that as a black person you can be killed for simply being black: no hands in your pockets, no playing music, no sudden movements, no driving your car, no walking at night, no walking in the day, no turning into this street, no entering this building, no standing your ground, no standing here, no standing there, no talking back, no playing with toy guns, no living while black."

(Claudia Rankine. "The Condition of Black Life Is One of Mourning." The New York Times, June 22, 2015[77])

Poverty and prison

While all Canadians who live beneath the poverty line are by no means associated with criminal activity, almost all those in Canada's prisons come from beneath the poverty line.

Less than 10 per cent of Canadians live beneath the poverty line but almost 100 per cent of our prison inmates come from that 10 per cent.

More than 70 per cent of those who enter prisons have not completed high school.

Seventy per cent of offenders entering prisons have unstable job histories.

Four of every five arrive with serious substance-abuse problems.

A Toronto study of 300 homeless adults found 73 per cent of men had been arrested and 49 per cent of them incarcerated at least once.

Twelve per cent of homeless women had served time.[78]

Majority of admissions to correctional services are younger adults[79]

In 2014/2015, adults under 35 years old accounted for 58% of admissions to provincial/ territorial corrections.

Findings for custodial admissions to federal correctional services were similar with the majority (54%) of adults admitted being under 35 years of age.

Young adults are overrepresented in admissions to adult correctional services given that individuals between 18 and 34 years of age represent 20% of the Canadian adult population.

CHAPTER TEN

WEDNESDAY, FEBRUARY 18

I've been giving writing workshops in the prison for over a year and have worked with people who have been accused of serious crimes that grievously harm other people but I have never been afraid of anyone in the workshops until I meet Lane. Because she has an unusual last name I know immediately why she is in jail. Her name has been in all the papers. She came east from across the country, and was accused of planning a terrorist attack. She wanted to kill as many innocent people as possible, people she did not know, most of them families enjoying themselves on a Sunday afternoon.

Lane is a woman in her early twenties and her long hair, which she'd dyed carrot red, looks unwashed and greasy. So does her face, which makes her appear unwell. Despite this, I would have thought of her as a pretty young woman had it not been for her eyes, which look dead. Her glazed eyes hold no emotion.

I hand out the poem "Her Kind" by Anne Sexton.[80] Even before I knew that Lane would be in the class, I chose Sexton because she was fearless in her poems, exploring mental illness, suicidal thoughts, her fraught relationships with her husband, and intimate details about her and her daughters. A Roman Catholic priest told her, "God is in your typewriter" and some critics believe writing gave the poet the willpower to continue living, though eventually she did take her life, when she was forty-five.

Years ago, I felt a strong urge to connect with Sexton and wrote the poem "Her Kind."[81] When I first wrote the poem a friend said, "You should write another stanza explaining what connects you to Anne."[82] I wrote the second stanza and the reasons I felt drawn to Anne surprised me: her intensity of feeling, her need to create. I longed to be as bold as she was. Then my friend said, "Now Anne has to respond to you!"

I took a long walk on the beach alone and asked Anne Sexton questions. And she responded. But my friend still did not think the poem complete. "Why don't you have a dialogue in the final stanza?" she suggested. The final lines in my poem came to me because I heard Anne Sexton say these words:

> ... *One day*
> *you'll be amazed how deep you'll go.*
> *You haven't yet told your story.*
> *You called on me to tell you this*
> *and I can: It's time. Nothing will pull you under.*

What generous reassurance Sexton offered. Though she was no longer alive, she was certainly alive to me when we spoke on the beach.

I told this story to participants in an earlier workshop on the East Wing, but with Lane in this workshop I am not comfortable talking so intimately. I say what first attracted me to Sexton's poems was her language and the wildness and daring of her subject matter, which contrasted with her tight rhyme scheme and meter.

In the workshop, we talk about the rhyme scheme and what the poet was writing about in the lines,

> *A woman like that is not a woman, quite.*
> *I have been her kind. ...*
> *A woman like that is misunderstood.*
> *I have been her kind.*

What does it mean to be seen as a woman who disappoints expectations? I ask participants in this workshop if they can write about a time they pretended they were fine but weren't.

Everyone is interested in doing the assignment but Lane.

I tell her that her last name is lovely and ask what the origin is. She mentions one of the poorer countries in Southeast Asia and tells me her mother is from there. Has she ever been there? She has, but a long time ago, in 2013. That is only a few years ago, I say. Does she want to write about family she visited there?

No.

Does she want to write about the countryside, the marketplace, her impressions of the landscape? No. I don't like to write about anything personal, she says.

She says she is writing a story and I tell her she is welcome to use her time in the workshop to work on it.

After fifteen minutes of writing, each woman

shares her piece. Lane's story has a lot of momentum and lively language but the subject matter alarms me. The main character, Bruno, kills two men because he thinks there is a possibility they might rape him, and then he dismembers them. I ask what she thinks about Bruno.

I don't know, she says.

Do you think there is anything wrong with him?

No, she says.

I tell her the story is well written, but I think the character has qualities of a psychopath. A psychopath is someone who has no conscience, who can murder those close to him, or strangers, and feel nothing, I say. I ask if she thinks the character is a psychopath.

She doesn't answer. Gabrielle, a woman in her early thirties, says, I think she has a bestselling novel here.

The superficiality of Gabrielle's response annoys me. I don't want to discuss commercial success. I want to talk about the moral implications. Lao Tzu says, "In dealing with others, do not judge." But it is hard not to judge. I know he is right, and still I am constantly judging.

I ask if there is a problem glorifying a character who has no conscience.

I wonder what Lane thinks of this comment. Lane is the first person I have met who I think might actually hurt me if she had the opportunity. I hope my intuition is wrong. I realize I would be relieved if she did not come to the workshop the following week, but she does come.

WEDNESDAY, FEBRUARY 25

I'd asked the women to write about addiction. The others have done the assignment, but not Lane.

Gabrielle says that she took drugs to forget what her childhood was like. She says her parents were drunk most of the time and violent. They were not involved in her life and never showed affection. She vowed she would be the opposite kind of parent when her sons were born. She believed that if she were affectionate, and involved in her sons' lives, they would not turn to drugs, but things didn't turn out that way. She starts to cry.

The judgement I had of Gabrielle the week before radically changes. And it will flip again as the weeks pass. Gabrielle is a challenge for me.

Alice writes that she had to have operations in her teens because she had a disease and problems with her bones. And then, in her twenties, her apartment caught fire and she had to jump from a third-storey window, which was the only way to escape. The fall was incredibly painful.

As she tells her story I look at Lane; her eyes are closed and she is smiling. It looks as if she is enjoying hearing Alice describe the pain she is in.

Alice writes that her doctor prescribed pain medication after that incident and she became addicted to opioids.

Afterwards I talk to the corrections officer on the women's wing. I tell her that Lane is the most detached, remote person I have ever worked with.

Yes, the CO says, she's crazy. Her heroes are mass murderers. When her parents drove all the way from

Calgary to visit her, she wouldn't see them. She refused to be assessed by a psychiatrist.

When I hear this I feel a knot of anxiety in my stomach. I wonder if Lane is a psychopath. Are you afraid of her? I ask.

Nah! the correction officer says.

But I am. I began giving workshops in the corrections facility because I believed writing was a way of healing. I soon realized I had as much to learn from the men and women I worked with as I had to offer. I still believe that the more time people take to reflect on experiences and the clearer they can be when they recall memories, the more lucid their thinking will become. I've been grateful to have the opportunity to encourage inmates and praise their work. Some have written moving, powerful pieces. But when I work with Lane, I don't believe I can be of any assistance. I question if art will help in any way. What can I do with this realization?

I call Jane, who edits a journal and is planning an issue devoted to women who are or have been incarcerated. She says she understands my fears. She says there should be someone in the prison to work with Lane. I think I know Lane in a way the COs might not, because I hear what she writes. It is difficult to hide what is on someone's mind when he or she is writing, whether the genre is fiction or non-fiction or poetry. But I am not a psychologist and do not have the skills to make an assessment.

Jane gives me the name of a woman she knows who is a psychologist teaching at a local university.

THURSDAY, MARCH 5

I hand out the poem "Has My Heart Gone To Sleep" by Antonio Machado.[83] I love Machado's ability to surprise, and to help readers hear the inner voice.

His "moral proverbs," as he calls them, wake me up:

> *It is good knowing that glasses*
> *are to drink from;*
> *the bad thing is not to know*
> *what thirst is for.*

And these wonderful lines:

> *Why should we call these accidental furrows roads?*
> *Everyone who moves,*
> *walks, like Jesus, on the sea.*

His proverb reminds me of these words by Thich Nhat Hanh:

> *the real miracle is not to walk,*
> *either on water or in thin air,*
> *but to walk on earth*

After reading Machado's poem I ask the women to write about someone they feel close to. Later I tell them that an editor I know who started an online journal is putting out an issue with pieces written by women in prison. I tell them I can email their work to the editor if they want. If they would rather not participate that's fine too. The editor may not accept their work, I say. I add, The purpose of the workshop is to explore experiences and write clearly about them. It is up to you if you want me to type up your stories and submit them.

The women want to participate. At the end of the session, four of the women are still working on their pieces and when they read them I suggest expanding their work in various ways: describe how the characters look, where the action takes place, how the character feels.

Mia has finished her piece. It is about her aging mother and young son. She describes what she remembers about her mother, the smell of tea rose soap her mother used, how beautiful she was. She says her son will remember her own thick unruly hair and when he has children and they grow up, they will remember what he was like when they were young.

I send it to Jane. I tell her my role is to encourage women to write, not to critique or edit their work as the workshop is only six weeks and I want it to be a positive experience for participants. The only suggestions I make are for women to give details so readers can visualize what is happening. But Jane is an editor of a journal and she can make further recommendations. The women understand these suggestions are supportive.

Jane proposes a few helpful changes for Mia's piece which I pass on to Mia at the next workshop.

THURSDAY, MARCH 12

On my way to the prison I am listening to the CBC Radio *Tell me a Story* when a podcast from *The Moth* is played.[84] It is about a woman whose mother is adventurous. She was born in Kansas, fell in love with a man from Nigeria whom she met at university. When he married her he said he would take her back to his country. But he did not take her back when he left. She remained in the U.S. with a two-year-old and a one-month-old. However, her daughter tells the audience, her mother never gave up her desire for adventure. Instead, her mother changed her definition of adventure. When the electricity was cut off, the family became campers in the middle of a forest. Again and again, Ejoma Elumu describes difficulties that would make most families despair. But Ejoma's mother found the fortitude to show her daughters that these hardships could actually be experienced as exciting escapades. My eyes tear up as I listen. I am happy to be alive. I know how lucky I am to be heading to the correctional facility to give a workshop.

THURSDAY, MARCH 19

Mia had to go to the methadone clinic so comes late to class. She says she is glad to be on methadone. She feels free. She is no longer a slave to drugs. She would like to be off methadone by the time her son is five, but if she has to be on it the rest of her life, that would be okay.

Gabrielle writes about her boyfriend, but her boyfriend, I learn, has murdered his ex-girlfriend. I thank her for writing the poem. I say she might want to explore why she was drawn to this person. If she were to warn her daughter not to get involved with a murderer, what would be the signs her daughter should look out for? I tell her she doesn't have to explore these questions, and if she does she doesn't have to share what she's written. But I encourage her to write about this as I think it will help her understand herself. What does she think?

She does not answer.

Mia does not have long to write her piece, as she came in late, and I am impressed by how quickly she completes the assignment. She writes,

SCARS

Having short sleeves in the summer may not seem frivolous but when your arms are covered in scars of psoriasis, new and old, wounds fresh and wounds old, wounds that are still to come, you begin to wear long sleeves as if they were your own skin.

A homeless man shouted at me from across the street as I was walking with my son, "Bed bugs! Bed bugs! Don't let the bed bugs bite that baby."

I wondered if he remembered that only a few days ago I gave him pocket change and cigarettes when he asked. He never even thanked me. So I ignored him and walked on.

Two days later I was arrested for shoplifting skin care products. The arresting officer wouldn't even touch me to put on cuffs. He borrowed gloves from a sales clerk who snorted in distaste at my appearance. I could almost reach out and touch the waves of hate and ignorance seeping from her very core.

Upon my arrival at the clink I was denied long sleeves at admission. After getting settled in, a girl in my day room handed me a long-sleeved shirt, told me her name and said simply, "I understand."

How unusual and lovely it was to me to find compassion in a person

```
who has obviously been condemned of
being anything but compassionate.
```

* * *

I show Mia the comments Jane made on her piece from the previous week. Jane says she thinks the piece is sensory and memorable: the smells, the texture, etc. I ask Mia if I can send Jane her piece "Scars" as well and she agrees.

I also ask Julia if I can send Jane her piece about celebrating Christmas with a needy family. Julia agrees. Although Julia's piece was in a newsletter, this is an on-line literary journal that has a wide readership.

Jane is very enthusiastic about Julia's piece as well.

Several months later Jane is ready to publish the online journal that focuses on writing from women who are or have been in prison. She has chosen to include Mia's piece, "Scars," but she hasn't heard back from her. Mia is no longer in prison. I email her Mia's father's number, which Mia wrote on her piece as contact information, and offer to try and make contact if Jane wants me to call.

Again she lets me know that she can't reach either Mia or Julia. She has undertaken an enormous job, there is only so much she can do, but I am disappointed to hear this.

Eventually Jane does reach Mia and publishes her piece. She has not been able to reach Julia.

I am grateful that Mia gets to see her name in print. How I want Julia to feel the pride of being published in this journal as well.

* * *

I am finally able to reach the professor who teaches psychology and who Jane suggested I call. I talk to her about Lane and tell her my fears that Lane may be a psychopath.

She may not be, the professor tells me. She says Lane may be pretending. Or she may have shut down but may still be reachable. This gives me some hope, even though the woman I speak to has never met Lane. The blind are leading the blind, but now there is a possibility we just might stumble upon a path, blind as we are.

How long can Lane be kept in prison if she did not actually commit the crime, but was caught planning it? Will she be let out without receiving any effective psychiatric attention, and with the same desire to kill as many innocent people as possible?

Our system seems to be reactive only, arresting those about to commit crimes (if the police are lucky enough to get a tip) or those who have already done great harm. Where are services to aid the mentally ill who have not yet acted out? I've heard podcasts in which parents talk about having no place to bring disturbed teenage sons and daughters so they can get much needed help for them. In some instances, there is no way to prevent these clearly deranged people from buying guns. It's a complicated problem and I don't pretend to understand the finances or politics of prevention. All I can do is bring poetry to the people locked inside.

Health care[85]

Mental illness, drug/alcohol addiction and infectious disease are the most prevalent health problems among offenders:

> Almost half of incoming male offenders have a alcohol dependence or substance use disorders.

> Nearly one-third of women offenders have previously been hospitalized for psychiatric reasons.

> 17% of the incarcerated population is infected with Hepatitis C.

The proportion of the inmate population over the age of 50 has grown to nearly 25%, an overall increase of nearly one-third in the last five years.

> The system is facing capacity and resource challenges to provide for the increased health care needs associated with aging, chronic illness and end-of-life care.

> The management of self-injurious, suicidal and mentally ill offenders continues to be met with security-driven responses including use of force, restraints and segregation.

(Office of the Correctional Investigator Annual Report 2014-2015 Backgrounder)

CHAPTER ELEVEN

WEDNESDAY, MARCH 25

The corrections officers said the guys on 6 West want a writing workshop. 6 West is the unit for sex offenders and I am nervous about working with these men. I mention this to Shiloh when I see her at the university and she says, I don't mind working with sex offenders. What I think she is saying is They are people too. They are humans with problems. I am not afraid that they will hurt me; what's more important, I believe I can be helpful to them. So I think, Okay, I can work with these men too. Later she says that yes, that is what she meant. Such is the benefit from talking with Shiloh, because her words ring true. Some of the men I meet in this workshop are amazing and I will never forget them.

And as soon as the five men walk into the room, all young, only one man who looks to be in his late thirties, I feel sympathy for them. Two men look like kids. I ask how old they are: twenty and twenty-two. I ask the men in the workshop their names. In other workshops some men make up names, Tiger or Shorty, and most do not include their last names. But all the men on 6 West tell me their first and last names and where they are from, when they introduce themselves.

The men in the workshop are Vaughn, Jerome, Brent, Nelson, and another Vaughn. They are from Pictou, Springhill, Yarmouth, Newfoundland, and a First Nations community in Cape Breton.

I give out Robert Frost's "Acquainted with the Night." I have learned that many participants in these workshops like rhyme and Frost uses rhyme so effectively. He is a master of atmosphere too.

> *Acquainted with the Night*[86]
> *by Robert Frost*
>
> *I have been one acquainted with the night.*
> *I have walked out in rain – and back in rain.*
> *I have outwalked the furthest city light.*
>
> *I have looked down the saddest city lane.*
> *I have passed by the watchman on his beat*
> *And dropped my eyes, unwilling to explain.*
>
> *I have stood still and stopped the sound of feet*
> *When far away an interrupted cry*
> *Came over houses from another street,*
>
> *But not to call me back or say good-bye;*
> *And further still at an unearthly height,*
> *One luminary clock against the sky*
>
> *Proclaimed the time was neither wrong nor right.*
> *I have been one acquainted with the night.*

As soon as we read the poem we are deep inside the lonely, rainy night Frost conjures in such few words. His poems seem simple on first reading, yet the appearance of simplicity is deceptive. Frost is a subtle and complex poet. Each time I return to his poems they offer more.

I ask what they think Frost was acquainted with, and what night represents.

Vaughn, who is in his thirties, says it means darkness, something you can't bring yourself to talk about. That is why you "drop your eyes."

That is so astute, I say.

Why is the time neither right nor wrong? I ask and when no one answers I say, Does it ever feel like the "right" time to gather our courage and confront the darkness, the unknown, all that "night" connotes?

We talk about obsessions, things that overwhelm us, how we are tempted to deny we have compulsions or refuse to admit their grip on us. Brent says you can't ignore them, you have to look them straight in the eye.

I ask the men to write about a time they acted like everything was fine when it wasn't. I say my sons are grown now but when my youngest was in fifth grade he went through a difficult time and lashed out, doing things that angered me. But the very act of pushing me away was a sign that he needed to talk with me. I was angry he punched holes in the walls, but when I finally realized he was in trouble and, instead of yelling at him, reached out to him, he eventually started crying and shared the pain he was feeling and what caused it. I was a single parent then and felt doubly responsible for how my children were feeling. I learned that often when someone pushes you away that is exactly when they want to get close to you, or need to be close with someone. This violent cycle, unless halted, inflicts a lot of harm.

Brent says he can relate to that because he keeps pushing away his wife. I ask why and he says many reasons. Brent is the oldest guy in the group, perhaps in his late thirties. The twenty-year-old Vaughn says he has been in Juvie since he was thirteen. Brent says he was in Juvie when he was eleven. Did I hear right? He does not want to read his story but he says it is okay for me to read it. This is what he writes:

```
IN-CLASS ASSIGNMENT by Brent

     When I was about 9 or 10 years
old, me and my baby sister Am-
ber were in our parent's room and I
was in their bed. My sister had our
mom's cigarette lighter and I took
it from her and I lit my parent's
room on fire, and threw the light-
er to my sister and told her not
to say nothing to mom or dad that I
did it, and if she did I would kill
her. So then I ran out to my room,
and played video games.
     The Smoke detector went off and
we went to the room where the smoke
was coming from. So then our dad got
the fire out and we went outside,
and after that my dad and mom asked
who it was who lit the fire. My
sister said she did it and took the
blame off me. Even to this day they
still don't know that I did it and
that is why I can't look my parents
in the eye when they ask me about
the fire.
```

I ask if he would consider writing a letter to his sister, apologizing to her. He says he can't do it. His sister is dead to him. He never speaks to her. He doesn't think she'd want anything to do with him either. She has children now. He doesn't.

I say to Brent, he was only eleven, just a kid, when

he set his parents' room on fire. He must have been so angry to do that. What made that little eleven-year-old boy so angry?

He says he wanted to kill his father, who was drunk all the time. His father would hit him and his mother and call him names. Then Brent says, And I was jealous of my sister. I wanted the family to be just my mother and me, not my sister.

The other men don't say anything. We sit in silence as his words sink in.

WEDNESDAY, APRIL 1

Brent does not return to the group. The CO says that he has gotten a job in the laundry. Later he does come by and explains that he feels better working in the laundry. That he is under a lot of stress and he does not want to delve into personal things in his writing. I am a man, he says, and men don't talk about personal things.

I say, I appreciate the courage it took to write what you wrote last week. But if you ever do return, you don't have to write personal stories, I tell him.

Neither of the Vaughns return today. As Jerome explains, someone complained about them and they were moved off the range.

Nelson is back. He hands me seven or eight pages he's written over the week, poems, prose pieces. His poems are so raw. He writes about horrible visions he has, demons in him that make him have distorted thoughts. He reads a poem out loud talking about these demons. He writes, "don't judge me by the way I look, don't judge me by the colour of my skin, don't judge me by the language I speak." The poem ends, "Who is going to care about a poor little Indian boy like me." I tell him how moving his poem is.

He talks about how he was in foster care with a family who were pretty crazy. He spoke only Mi'kmaq at the time but none of the other foster kids spoke it so he was not allowed to speak his language. The other kids bullied him. They called him names. He was angry and hurt much of the time and had no one to confide in.

I hand out the Langston Hughes' poem "A Dream Deferred,"[87] and when I say the title Howard says he can relate to that. Howard is a new member of the group. He is a large Black man in his late forties, early fifties. I ask him to explain and he says that even though he served his country for fourteen years and worked for his community, now that he is in jail all that is cancelled. He can't have the dreams he once had.

I say, I understand how he feels, but there are people who have been in jail and after they are released they have useful lives and are helpful in their community.

He says he has to be realistic. Once people know you have been in jail, they treat you differently, he says. You can't get a job at most places if you've been a convict. He does not say why he is here. He does not acknowledge why people who are sexual offenders are treated differently by the outside world than other convicts.

We read "When Leather is a Whip,"[88] by Martín Espada, a poem that elicited powerful responses in previous workshops in other wings of the prison. The men explain the poem right away – a man does not want to remind his wife of the days when she was little and her father was cruel and whipped her, so he turns away from her when he is undressing so she won't see him taking off his belt.

I ask the men to write about a time when they were kind to someone or someone was kind to them, as the man in the poem was kind to protect his wife. Or they can write about a time they were unkind to someone or someone was unkind to them, a more difficult assignment.

Howard writes about growing up in a large family. He had fifteen brothers and sisters. In order to make a little money he would sell papers in the neighbourhood. Many of his neighbours could not read, yet they would buy a paper from him anyway, to be supportive. His eyes fill with tears and his voice breaks as he remembers what his community did for him. I say I feel his big heart and his powerful feelings. It is great to hear this story, I tell him. He writes that he would try to read articles to some of these people but he could not understand the big words. Once he stole a dictionary from school and when he was reading articles to his neighbours he would look up words. Earlier, when we read "A Dream Deferred," he asked me what "deferred" meant.

Carter, a man in his late twenties, neat, handsome, with a close-shaven beard, is also new to the group. He writes that he always wanted to be a mechanic. When he was growing up, his family did not have money and when their car broke down, his father would fix the car himself. Carter would watch and was always interested in the mechanics of cars. He is married now; he met his future wife when he was in junior high. Her father repaired cars and when Carter married his daughter, he paid for Carter to go to trade school to learn to be a mechanic. Then he hired Carter to work with him. Carter has always been grateful to his father-in-law for this.

I wonder what crime he committed that brought him here. I ask if he is still married. Yes, he says. Is he still working for his father-in-law? His father-in-law is dead, he says, and he is working for someone else now.

Carter is polite, low-key, but he is also removed, as if he is surrounded by fog.

Jerome says he wrote a poem and reads about a woman he helped on the bus and how she appreciated his help. Why did she need help? Was she old and had difficulty walking? Was she young with many packages? What was the weather like, what was she wearing? What did she look like? I say it is the details that make a poem or prose piece come alive. Jerome says he did not know he needed details in a poem. I say the more specific he makes his writing, the more alive it will be. It is a paradox that the more detailed he is about his particular experiences, the easier it will be for readers to access their own experience. He says he will rewrite the poem and add details.

The next morning I wake up to seagulls screeching on my roof. What are they fighting about? What caused this morning insurrection?

WEDNESDAY, APRIL 8

Howard does not return. He was in court and got bad news and is upset. Perhaps he is embarrassed as well because he cried during the last session. The CO tells me that he says he will come next week. We'll see.

Nelson is not here. The men say he is in court. Today Carter, Jerome, and the older Vaughn return, and two new members, Marshall and Glen. Marshall is a heavy man in his fifties, close in age to Howard, but Marshall grew up in rural Nova Scotia. Glen is in his early twenties.

I ask the men to write about a teacher who was kind or one who was unkind during their school years. When I gave this exercise on the North Wing the men wrote about teachers who were cruel, nuns who mistreated them at residential schools, teachers who whipped them with rods. But all the men on 6 West write about teachers who were kind.

Marshall, the middle-aged, heavyset man, writes about a math teacher he had when he was in eighth grade. He loved math and the teacher encouraged him. Marshall also loved Cadillacs and the teacher had a blue Cadillac he knew Marshall admired. The teacher told Marshall that if he got over a ninety on his exam he could drive his Cadillac and Marshall did get over ninety. Did he get to drive the car? He did, he says. And he was only fourteen. But in the rural area where he lived, many fourteen-year-olds knew how to drive. He said the teacher gave out a riddle – If an eighteen-wheeler was stuck under a bridge, how would you get it out? Marshall said, I was the only one who knew the answer: let the air out of the tires.

Jerome says his fifth grade teacher was nice to him. He could talk to her about anything, what was bothering him at home, why he was upset. She always had time for him. The only thing was, she wanted him to go with her daughter, and he didn't want to. He was only in fifth grade. Did the teacher really want him to date her daughter? Something is odd here but I don't say anything.

Vaughn says that his eighth grade teacher was the nicest teacher he ever had. Every week she would take the four best students to the movies and to an Italian restaurant. He never got to go but she said if he tried hard one week she would take him and she did. He could order anything he wanted at the restaurant. It was a great treat for him. What a nice teacher, he says. She wasn't married, she had no children, and she devoted a lot of time to her students.

I wonder if these teachers know their acts of kindness are remembered decades later, especially by students who were treated harshly by their families, group homes, communities.

Jerome says that he lived in a group home when he was in high school and it was hard for him to bridge the gap between this group home and school. But he had a teacher, a white guy who was a fan of hip hop, and he liked this teacher.

I hand out the poem "Late Fragment" by Raymond Carver.[89] It's a short poem. A voice in the poem asks the poet if he got what he wanted in this life. The poet says he did. These are the last three lines of the poem:

> *And what did you want?*
> *To call myself beloved, to feel myself*
> *beloved on the earth.*

I ask the men if they feel loved. Glen says he is young, only in his twenties, and he thinks he can be loved. I say that being loved is a birthright everyone is entitled to. The talk evolves into what the men would like to do in their lives.

Marshall writes that he likes to help people. When he gets out he wants to be a paramedic. He would like to be helpful in prison too, he says, because there are people here who are guilty, but there are people here who aren't guilty. Even in prison he feels he has a good life, he says. He can be kind to people, buy them something from the canteen. He says, I've lived my life. I'm happy.

What does he mean he's lived his life? Looking at this man who has been arrested as a sexual predator, I wonder, as I do about so many of the men here, was he a victim of a predator as well?

Carter writes about building a shack with his cousin who was his best friend and still is. Now they are building a playhouse for his children and his cousin's children. He loves doing this in his spare time. He will be out in a few months.

The man has a very insular life: marries a girlfriend he had since seventh grade, his best friend is his cousin, his affect is dull. Not that he is not bright, but to me it seems that something comes between him and the world. What trauma has he undergone and what trauma has he caused?

WEDNESDAY, APRIL 15

I wake up to news on the radio announcing that a prisoner was beaten on his first day at the Nova Scotia Correctional Facility and is in the hospital with a swollen brain. His mother is only allowed to visit him an hour a day. She is in tears when she is interviewed; her son is in danger, she wants to be with him during the entire day, not just for one hour.

This news is painful to hear. If one of my sons had been attacked and was in hospital fighting for his life, I would want to stay by his side. To have to leave each day after an hour visit would be unbearable.

In the workshop at the facility later that day, I hand out the poem "Back to the Machine Gun" by Charles Bukowski.[90] Bukowski is a wild man. *Time* magazine called him "the laureate of American lowlife" in 1986. The critic Michael Greenberg described his work as "a detailed depiction of a certain taboo male fantasy: the uninhibited bachelor, slobby, anti-social, and utterly free."[91] He is so different than Robert Frost, whose work we discussed in our last workshop. Though Bukowski died in 1994, his poems read as if they were written recently. I am curious how this poem will go over, and ask the men what they think the poem means.

They say it is about a loser, coming off a drunk. Jerome says this poem is more contemporary than the other poems I gave out. I say, Yes, it is about someone who has a hangover. When he hears his neighbour's voice calling out *Good morning*, it is almost like

> *being shot in the ass*
> *with a .22*

because of his headache from that hangover. Yet he is able to describe what he feels in great detail. I tell the men that for the next assignment I want them to in-clude details that affect all their senses: what they hear, see, touch, smell, and taste.

They tell me they have done their homework from last week and have written about a time they were happy.

Glen writes about being with his grandfather,

delivering mail and being allowed to drive his grand-father's car, which he'd wanted to drive.

Jerome says his piece is six pages long. I say perhaps he can condense this piece, as there are six participants who have to read their work. He slams the pages on the table and says forget it, he won't read at all. What is the point of writing the homework if he can't read it? What sort of creative writing course is this, any-way? Nelson says he has a long piece too. I ask if he can start reading it and we'll see how much time we have. He says he doesn't want to summarize it, but he doesn't want to have a fit like Jerome. At this, Jerome gets up and says he wants to leave and can we get a guard. The group spends some time trying to calm Jerome down. I tell him I'd like him to stay.

We listen to Nelson's piece about something that made him happy. His stepsister said his stepbrother was coming to visit. His stepbrother hadn't visited in a long time and she asked Nelson if he was okay with the visit. Nelson said he was, and then under his breath muttered, It's his funeral. When his stepbrother came, he beat him up, elephant-stomped him, threw him down the steps. Then he called the ambulance. His step-brother was in a coma for months. Nelson writes, That was a happy time, beating him up.

I ask why he was so angry. He says his step-brother, who was six years older than him, had sexually assaulted him when he was young. I say I can understand why he was so angry but isn't there another way to deal with this? What if he had killed the man and had to spend years in prison? What a waste of his life that would have been.

I ask Nelson if he would still beat someone up if that person wronged him and he says no, he knows who he is now, he has been in touch with his roots and the elders and he has Jesus in his life. He knows there is another way to handle anger. But then, he didn't know. And no, he is not sorry he beat him up. His stepbrother deserved it, after what he did.

He speaks passionately. He is not a hypocrite; he knows who he is. And though I should not condone his actions, I can't help but understand his point of view. I like Nelson. If he is given opportunities, I am certain his strengths and talents will flourish. I am reminded of George Saunders' words: "It is as if that is the point of power: to allow one to access the higher registers of gentleness."[92]

Marshall says, I have a daughter and if she were sexually assaulted I would tell her to do the same thing. Now Jerome reads his story, which goes on and on. He repeats himself and the writing is hard to follow. The time allotted for the workshop is running out. I will not be able to give a homework assignment. Finally I say, Jerome, thank you for writing this long piece, but in order for us to finish the workshop on time and for me to give the assignment, you'll have to summarize your piece or read the rest next week.

Again he tells me I don't know how to lead a workshop. How is he supposed to learn how to write if he doesn't get feedback? What do I think of the piece? Jerome asks, What kind of a course is this, anyway? He never took creative writing in university but he says he has two degrees and this is sort of a psychology course. And it is true, I do want to get participants talking about their thoughts and feelings. Poetry has many layers, I say. Poetry makes the invisible visible. Reading poems is a way of encountering what is not on the surface.

Sebastian, the social work student, explains to Jerome that there are six men in the workshop and in order for everyone to have a turn, we have to share the time fairly. Jerome shoots back, You think you'll be a social worker, but in the group home I was in, they would eat you alive.

Look, I say, Sebastian has been so generous with his time; he comes here once a week to assist me. But Sebastian says he does not want me to defend him.

A difficult day in the prison. After the men leave, the CO tells me she always compliments Jerome so he won't go off the rails. When Sebastian and I are alone I say, Perhaps we should ask the corrections officer not to invite Jerome back. He is so disruptive. I don't think I can help him. And he takes so much time away from discussions.

But Sebastian thinks we should let him return. He says, Guys in jail are used to people giving up on them. Sebastian is right. I learn a lot from him.

The following week, the CO emails to tell me the prison is under lockdown. Then I go to New York to visit family so do not get back to the workshop for two weeks.

WEDNESDAY, MAY 6

I hand out certificates that state the writing workshop has been completed. Nelson wants two certificates. I tell him he doesn't need two.

I ask the men to pretend decades have passed and they are writing a letter as older men to themselves at the age they are now, helping themselves with a problem they are having. I suggest that they have the answer, inside them, to their current difficulties.

That's weird, Jerome says.

I have no problems, Nelson says.

I feel crazy writing to myself, Glen says.

I say, You know how we tell ourselves negative things – What a jerk I am. How stupid of me. Now, instead of insults, you can say positive things to yourself and can explain to yourself how you can be helpful.

Glen says he'll write but he won't share what he's written. I ask if I can read it and he says no. I want to know why and he says what he is writing is inappropriate. I say, If you are honest, why is it inappropriate? Glen says this is his problem and he is trying to work it out. Then Jerome says, I know what it is.

Perhaps Glen is writing about a sexual fetish or sexual aggression. I am glad he is writing. And I finally clue in that I should not ask prying questions.

Nelson writes that he is puzzling and baffling, that he is funny-looking, that he is spoiled fruit.

I say fruit that is spoiled can't be saved. Nelson says, You can dry fruit or hydrate it and it is fine. Nelson is so smart.

I am sorry he says he is funny-looking. When I first saw him, I thought he was funny-looking too. He has a large mouth, big ears. But now I love to look at Nelson, who has so much heart, and who is so obviously beautiful.

When I ask the men to share what they wrote last week, about their father or mother, or an adult they spent a lot of time with, Nelson says, You were away so long, I sent what I wrote to my woman.

I tell him I am glad to hear that.

I thank the men for taking the workshop and Glen says, Thank *you*. Then Nelson says, Hey, wait a minute. You've been coming here for six weeks and you never shared anything you wrote.

I tell them I am happy to read a poem I wrote. They ask if I have books and I bring out the poetry books and children's books I wrote and which I carry in my supply bag. If participants ask to see books I've written, I like to share them because being a published writer may lend more weight to the compliments I give their work.

I read "Left." Jerome says, My favourite line is *The body is an alibi when the mind roams.*

I say, I wrote that poem about my friend Michael who had a hard life. He had a colostomy when he was sixteen and had to deal with his body being disfigured at such a young age. He died in his fifties of ALS, a disease where your mind remains healthy but the body slowly becomes paralyzed until finally the patient is unable even to swallow. Michael is dead now, but he was so generous to me when he was alive. I say, I think he is still helping me. The poem received a prize and I think Michael, even though he is on the other side, had a hand in that.

I am touched the men want to hear my poems. They ask if I make money from my books.

No, I tell them. But good things come from writing poems. I get to travel, and to teach.

Can you give us these books? they ask.

I don't have extra copies, I say, but you can get them from the library.

The local library? they ask.

Yes, I say. But they cannot get to the local library, of course.

I should have been more generous and gotten more copies of my books.

When we are about to leave, Nelson says again, So you are not going to give me two certificates? No! I say. Then he hands me the envelope of certificates I'd brought. He'd managed to swipe the entire envelope without my noticing. He has nimble fingers.

Marshall hands me a poem he wrote in class about Mrs. Langille, the professor. He says he wishes he could study at Dalhousie. I too wish he could study at Dalhousie University. But that's not going to happen. It costs a lot even to take a single course and there are academic requirements. What will the future hold for Marshall, and for the other men?

Overrepresentation of Indigenous people in Canada's prisons persists amid drop in overall incarceration[93]

"'Often ... disclosing an Indigenous background in prison can make it harder for inmates to access services,' ... said Robert Henry, an assistant professor at the University of Calgary who studies Indigenous issues in justice and education.

"... Though a number of complex factors are involved – such as poor access to education, media portrayal of Indigenous people as criminals and the lingering effects of residential schools – Henry said he believes a major one is the 'pipeline' of Indigenous youth moving from the child welfare system into the prison system. Removing children from families, he said, introduces instability that has consequences down the line.

"'We shouldn't be surprised that we're seeing more Indigenous people being incarcerated, because they're already being removed at such young ages and being institutionalized,' Henry said.

"'The attitude as I see it is that these people are gonna go to jail, they committed crimes and they belong in jail. That's what I hear in response to the high numbers. I want that attitude changed,' said Muriel Stanley Venne, president and founder of the Institute for the Advancement of Aboriginal Women in Edmonton.

" ... Henry said reforming the child welfare system would also be a natural way to start fixing the issue.

"These numbers aren't surprising, but with serious time and effort they need not be inevitable, Venne said. Many measures to improve the situation going forward have been identified by the TRC [Truth and Reconciliation Commission] and others, Venne said, but she hasn't seen a change in attitude.

"'This way, they're just building more jails,' she said. 'And we know who's going to be in those jails.'"

CHAPTER TWELVE

WEDNESDAY, MAY 13

I arrive at the prison at 1:50. The guard talks to the CO on his phone and then says, Send her through.

I buzz one locked door; it opens. Buzz another; it opens. I pass through a door and turn right. There is a locked gate, but no indication this is the North Wing. I retrace my steps, ask a guard. Yes, the sign is down but the North Wing is through that door. Ah, the sign is down. When I walk along these corridors, I feel like I'm in a maze, but now I don't judge myself so harshly for my difficulty in getting where I want to go.

Molly, the CO, a young woman who has recently returned from a year's maternity leave, and whom I am meeting for the first time, says she will get the men. She returns in a little while to tell me that since the workshop is during their exercise time, they don't want to come, even though she said she would reschedule exercise time. She said, I told the guys that the lady has driven an hour to get here, but they said if they didn't want to come, they didn't have to and stormed out.

I ask her to tell the men to come briefly so I can give them an assignment for the following week. When they do come I say I am sorry two things were scheduled during this time and we decide Thursdays at 1:30 will not interfere with any activity. I ask the men if I can give them a poem and an assignment and they say yes.

I hand out Suzanne Buffam's poem "On Attachment."[94] It begins, *A house burns all night* and ends,

> *Sooner or later*
> *All burning houses will be mine.*

The men ask if this is about people who burn houses. I say I think it's about how, ultimately, everything is temporary, even our lives. Sooner or later we must give up everything. And that is what connects us all, that we are all in the same predicament. Though you are in jail and I'm not, we are related. What affects one person affects us all, though we may not recognize this immediately.

Then I hand out sayings from Thich Nhat Hanh and we discuss, along with other quotes, *My actions are my only true belongings. I cannot escape the consequences of my actions. My actions are the ground on which I stand.*

Their assignment is to write about someone they thought of as their enemy but now find it possible to forgive.

THURSDAY, MAY 21

Remy, Owen, Ethan, Lynton are here.

Stephan can't come as he is "on the level." This is prison parlance for lockdown. I give out Maya Angelou's poem "Alone,"[95] which has the lines,

> *That nobody,*
> *But nobody*
> *Can make it out here alone*

I ask the men if they can describe a situation when they needed to ask for help but didn't or weren't heard when they did ask.

Owen says he never asks for help. I ask him to be specific. He says maybe he needs money. He could go to his aunts. They have some money and would give him some. But instead he goes to the store, lifts something, and sells it.

I invite the men to write about asking for help. They should write about what the situation was, who they asked, and the response. I also want them to write as if they were in a position to help and what their answer would have been to their own request. This is a bit confusing.

I should imagine a friend asking for help? Quentin says.

No. Imagine you are asking yourself for help. As if you have the remedy for what you should do.

Remy reads what he wrote. He stole $3,000 from his stepdad to buy crack. Then he went to his stepdad and said he needed help. At first his stepdad was angry, but then he brought Remy to rehab and said Remy could pay him back when he was clean. And Remy did pay him back. He got out of rehab, worked as a cook, and reimbursed him.

Owen says, You're just gonna start using again if you hang out with guys who do drugs.

I ask if he can get new friends and not hang out with the old friends. He says, It's hard and Owen says,

It just takes discipline. I thank Remy for writing such an honest, moving piece.

Owen writes how his girlfriend kicked him out, Because of damn lies people told her. He asked his brother Andre if he could live with him and he would pay rent and food. Andre said sure, but Andre's woman was a bitch and came between them. Now he is not speaking to Andre. He wishes his brother would break up with his woman. She called him to invite him over last Christmas, as if everything could be swept under the rug, but he told her he couldn't stand her.

At this point I say, Any thoughts about how Owen could handle this situation?

Ethan says, It's not your business who your brother is with. You have to make peace. I used to get angry all the time, but now I just let things be.

Owen says, I was just telling her how I felt, that I couldn't stand her.

I remind him of the Thich Nhat Hanh quote we read last week: *Letting go gives us freedom, and freedom is the only condition for happiness. If, in our heart, we still cling to anything – anger, anxiety, or possessions – we cannot be free.*

Owen says, I'm not holding on to anger, and Ethan says, Yes you are.

I ask them to read the two other quotes from Thich Nhat Hanh, again: *My actions are my only true belongings. I cannot escape the consequences of my actions. My actions are the ground on which I stand.*

And *When another person makes you suffer, it is because he suffers deeply within himself, and his suffering is spilling over. He does not need punishment; he needs help. That's the message he is sending.*

The men say they prefer to write in class so I do not give an assignment this week. But I say if they feel like it they can write about a nice deed they did during the week. Lynton says he helped an inmate read a letter and Remy says he helped him write a letter as the guy couldn't read or write.

THURSDAY, MAY 28

Remy, Owen, Ethan, Lynton are here today.

Owen says William, the man who I gave an assignment to at the first workshop when he didn't want to miss any of his exercise time, is in court. I say, I am glad you guys could come.

Remy says this may be his last week, as he thinks he is getting out next week. Remy is sitting at the same table as Owen, and puts his arm around Owen in a brotherly clasp. They laugh and seem to be good friends. When Remy starts writing he asks how to spell throat. Then he says, I'm not much of a writer. I saw someone's throat slit.

Then he reads his story. He was young. He doesn't remember how old. He saw his uncle's throat slit. He thought, Wow, that is a lot of blood. His aunt was crying and trying to help her husband.

Was he your mother's brother or your father's brother? I ask, and Remy says he doesn't know. I ask where his parents were.

They were dead, he says.

Did the police come? I ask.

Yes, and they took me and my brother away to foster care. I had a dog, but they did not let me take my dog.

You have been through so much, I say. Lawmakers seem to act in a vacuum when it comes to running prisons, I think. How much do they know about the people who end up here? I say, I am sorry you've suffered so much.

In his novel *Open City*, Teju Cole said, "... sometimes it is hard to shake the feeling that ... there really is an epidemic of sorrow sweeping our world, the full brunt of which is being borne, for now, by only a luckless few."[96] Ever since I read his words I feel he is an invisible observer in these workshops.

Ethan writes about how when his mother went out and his older brother babysat, his brother would sometimes beat him up with a baseball bat, pour water over him, lock him in a cage they had for the dog. I ask why his brother was such a sadistic bully and Ethan says, It wasn't any different than any other family.

I ask, Would you want your son to be beaten like that? and he says, I would want my son to defend himself. I wouldn't want my son to be weak or soft.

Later I hand out quotes by Joseph Campbell. Remy gets *The privilege of a lifetime is being who you are.* I say, Can you read it again? No one else has had your life or knows what you know because of the experiences you've had.

Owen gets *The cave you fear to enter holds the treasure you seek.*

What is the cave you fear to enter? I ask. I don't know, he says. Maybe love.

That is a powerful answer, I say, then add, I think there is strength in being vulnerable. I have two sons and I have always told them, It's good to cry. I think it's difficult to be a man in this world because men are told to hide how they feel.

When it is Remy's turn again he reads the quote, *When we quit thinking primarily about ourselves and our own self-preservation, we undergo a truly heroic transformation of consciousness.*

We talk about this. Remy says he tried to help his daughters, but his ex won't even let him see them.

But that is not the end of the story, I say. If their well-being comes first, you can figure out a way to serve them.

I try to. I bought them clothes for school but their mother told me to leave.

I tell him he'll have other opportunities to be generous with his children.

He says, My ex-wife won't let me near them.

Yes, I say, impatiently. I say, I don't want to hear about her.

At this Remy gets angry. He stops talking. I say, I didn't mean to offend you, and Remy says, Forget it, move on.

Had I forgotten so quickly about the trauma Remy wrote about? Why didn't I have a little more patience with him?

Ethan talks next. He reads the quote, *Sit in a room and read and read and read. And read the right books by the right people. Your mind is brought onto that level, and you have a nice, mild, slow-burning rapture all the time.* Ethan asks what "rapture" means. I say it means to feel great pleasure and delight. Have you heard music, or read a book or seen a movie you feel passionate about and that makes you feel elated?

The men don't answer. Then I say, Write a sentence with the word "rapture" in it.

"I feel rapture when I ..."

Remy will not write. I see his jaw clenching and unclenching. He is erasing something on the outside of his notebook. I say again I am sorry I was impatient with him. He has been through so much.

Lynton writes he feels rapture when he is cooking a delicious meal and when the patrons in the restaurant compliment him, it is better than any tip.

Great sentence, I say. The CO suggests he should try to be on *The Best Canadian Baking Show*.

Owen says he feels rapture when he is with his niece and nephew.

How nice is that! I say. I ask Remy if he has a sentence and he says, No. I am about to tell him I'd like him to try and write something when Owen says, Ethan, do *you* have a sentence? Owen knows this is not the time to try to get through to Remy. I appreciate that Owen is showing me how to be tactful and to move on.

Ethan says, I feel rapture when I am playing basketball. He says he was the captain of his team, that he once scored forty-seven baskets in one game. That's impressive, I say.

When we go around the room again, sharing quotes, Remy won't participate. I say again, I'm sorry, Remy, for upsetting you. I was wrong to speak the way I did.

I ask Ethan to read the quote by Thich Nhat Hanh about letting go of anger. Remy is still grinding his teeth. How is he going to manage on the outside, when he gets so angry by my impatience, and will not accept my apology? I wanted to explain that blaming someone else gets tiring, that all we can do is manage our own actions. But I lost my patience, so missed my opportunity.

Molly, the CO, asks Remy if he wants to leave and he says yes, and jumps up, and she gets one of the guards to lead him back. We finish the workshop, but I feel terrible that I failed him. The men and I talk about how, when we hold on to anger, it poisons not the person we are angry at, but ourselves.

Is there a chance something good will come out of this? I tell the CO that if Remy does not get out of prison this week, she should let him know he is welcome to return to the workshop again.

The CO says Remy is often angry but this wasn't so bad. She says she's seen him throw over tables. Poor young man. What chance does he have in the outside world? I ask her.

She says she doesn't think he has much of a chance. There are no resources in the prison to help him.

Later I tell my husband that I feel bad about what happened. I say, I apologized three times and he did not accept my apology. My husband says, Maybe on some level he did accept your apology. He just wanted to save face. And anger allowed him to release some of his pent-up feelings. I feel better hearing this. I have many people in my life who advise and support me. But who does Remy have?

I email my friend Sally with the details and she says, Even when we provoke the stuff that is not so pleasant, even when people shut down or run away, there is something real happening, an experience to learn from, if not today then maybe some other time.

And that's the gift of honest conversations. Sometimes great gifts have ugly wrappings.

Her words are helpful. Though I know, had I been more patient, the interaction would have been so much more productive for Remy and for me.

THURSDAY, JUNE 4

There are only three inmates here today: Owen, Lynton, and Stephan, who is in the workshop for the first time. Ethan was sentenced and transferred to Cape Breton. Remy is no longer in prison. The CO said she did not have time to ask if anyone else was interested in creative writing. Some of these guys don't want anything to do with any programs, she said.

I was hoping she would mention the workshop, and see who was interested. I am disappointed she does not give them the option, but it turns out the small group works well.

We read "Oranges"[97] by Gary Soto which begins,

> *The first time I walked*
> *With a girl, I was twelve,*
> *Cold, and weighted down*
> *With two oranges in my jacket.*

We talk about how powerful it is to care for someone, and how feelings are especially intense the first time you fall in love.

Then we read "ICU" by Spencer Reece.[98] He is another poet who makes me want to work harder and write deeper poems. How does he manage to reveal so much about his inner and outer world in so few words? Reece sent his manuscript to contests and publishers for about thirteen years and was rejected over three hundred times. He was over forty when his manuscript, *The Clerk's Tale*, was published after winning a contest. He continued to work full-time at a clothing shop in a mall though his book was highly praised by critics. When he won several fellowships and grants, he cut down his working hours and started volunteering in a hospice. Then he says he felt called; he went to Yale Divinity School and, after he became an ordained Episcopal priest, he began working as a chaplain. "Each door I open at Hospice, I move closer to something brightly intimate," he writes.[99]

When I ask the inmates why Reece's poem has the line, *their faces resigned in their see-through attics,* about infants in the ICU, Stephan says, Attic is the top of the house, or the top of the body, where the face is, and an infant in the ICU has transparent skin, maybe.

How smart Stephan is.

We talk about the line, *It is correct to love even at the wrong time.* The title of the poem, "ICU," is an acronym for Intensive Care Unit but what else might the poet be conveying with that title? I ask. One of the men says, in a tentative voice, I see you, like look at you? These men are sharp.

I ask the men to write about someone who cared about them and/or who they cared about and describe an interaction that showed that compassion.

Stephan writes about his favourite teacher from grade twelve who helped him when his father kicked him out. He'd stolen a case of beer from his dad and his dad's girlfriend. Stephan writes, My dad had to choose her or me and he chose her. Then Stephan called his teacher because he didn't know what to do. He decided he was going to move to P.E.I. because he had family there. That night his teacher got him a hotel room and the next morning she came and picked him up and paid for his bus ticket to P.E.I. and gave him $100 cash.

Even after I moved back from Charlottetown, Stephan says, there were a few times she took me to dinner and drove me around.

I ask Stephan where his mother was and he says she'd left long ago, when he was eight. I ask why his father kicked him out and he says, I was bad.

Owen says, I wish my mother had kicked me out. Maybe then things would have been different. She was always giving me a pass.

If she kicked you out, maybe you would have gotten into more trouble, Stephan says.

Most likely, Owen says. She always tells me, You can't fight fate. I love my mom though.

I asked these men what they need so they will not find themselves in jail again.

A lot of money, Owen says. Then he says, No, that isn't it. If I had a good woman, she could keep me out of prison. There are some things you can't forgive. Like Lynton's brother slept with his woman. I could not forgive that.

I quote a phrase I'd read in books by Pema Chödrön and Anne Lamott: "Holding onto anger is like drinking poison and expecting the other person to die."

But there are some things you can't forgive, Owen says. I went to a therapist three days a week when I was young and it didn't help.

You were very angry, I say.

No, I was acting out.

But weren't you acting out because you were angry?

Well, maybe I was. Maybe I was angry because my father was never there. My mother tried her best but she had three sons and she couldn't handle us all.

A lot is going on with you, I say. A lot is going on with all of you. Though this may not be a comfort to hear now, I think you have the answers. I tell them I am reminded of Lao Tzu's words, *At the center of your being you have the answer; you know who you are and you know what you want.*

THURSDAY, JUNE 11

Stephan is here and Owen. Lynton is having some of his teeth pulled so he can't attend. They say Curtis wanted to come but he is in class. I don't know if this is an anger management class, or a class to get his GED. Then he passes by. The door is locked, and the CO must buzz to get it opened. She does open it and sticks her head out the door. Do you want to come to a creative writing workshop, she asks. No answer. Then I go into the hall and say, Join us. And he does.

I give out "The Kindness of the Blind" by Wislawa Szymborska.[100] It is a poem about a poet reading his work to people who are blind. The narrator of the poem realizes, as he reads, that the audience will not be able to visualize any of the references, and becomes agitated. The poem ends,

> *Yet great is the kindness of the blind,*
> *great their compassion and generosity.*
> *They listen, smile, and clap.*

One of them even approaches
with a book held topsy-turvy
to ask for an invisible autograph.

Stephan says, I like that she says they're kind. I never thought of that.

We read Tony Hoagland's poem "Beauty" as well. I ask the men to write about someone who was kind to them, or to whom they were kind. The CO says she will write the exercise too.

Stephan writes about asking his father for money so he could join the pool at the Y and go swimming and his father said, Go out and earn it. So he began asking people in the neighbourhood if they needed their lawns mowed. One family invited him for dinner. Then they asked how much it would cost for him to join the pool. Fifty dollars. They insisted on giving him fifty dollars though he did not want to take it. They were very generous and that too was beautiful.

Owen writes about how he wanted to go to summer camp but his family couldn't afford it. Then he was having dinner with his friend and his friend's grandmother and later he found out that she paid for him to go to summer camp. He had a great summer! He said it cost $5,000 for the summer. Could it have been that much? Hard to believe. Perhaps, being young, he confused the sum. I get teary as these men talk about how kind their neighbours were. The CO is teary too.

Curtis writes about how a friend of his wrote him a letter from the future. She wrote, You were in jail for stealing cars, but now you own fancy cars and are in a great place. That letter too was beautiful.

I write about the time I lost patience with Remy and told him I didn't want to hear him blame his ex-wife. Remy was angry with me and refused to participate when everyone read a sentence about rapture. I was about to press him when Owen shifted the tension by asking another inmate, Okay, Ethan, what did you write? I say that Owen wanted to give Remy space and make sure we didn't focus on him when he clearly did not want to participate. I learned something from Owen, I say, and appreciate his sensitivity. That too was beautiful.

Owen smiles.

THURSDAY, JUNE 18

Owen, Curtis, and Lynton are here. Stephan has been released from prison.

I give out certificates as it is the last day of the workshop. Curtis asks if he can have a certificate, though he was only here two sessions. He asks if he can do extra work. It always surprises me that a piece of parchment paper that says a six-week course has been completed is so valuable, but in prison it is, so I list exercises Curtis can do. Then I sign the certificate and give it to the corrections officer to give to Curtis once he completes the assignments.

We talk about the murders at the Emanuel African Methodist Episcopal Church in South Carolina – nine people killed including the Rev. Clementa C. Pinckney, who was the church pastor and a prominent state senator. We talk about Pope Francis's encyclical, which said revolution was needed to combat climate change.

I hand out the poem "You Learn"[101] by Luis Borges. I ask why Borges says,

> And you begin to accept your defeats
> With your head up and your eyes open
> With the grace of a woman, not the grief of a child ...

Yeah, Owen says, why a woman, not a man?

There are many qualities men have that are admirable, I say. But accepting defeat is not an action encouraged for men in our society. Though it should be. It is a mark of maturity, the poet implies. Can we admire qualities the poet thinks women have, as the poet admires them?

Today I ask if the men in the workshop ever felt in danger in this prison. No, they say. Owen says he has felt he was in danger outside, on the streets, but not in here.

Borges writes,

> And you learn that you really can endure ...
> That you really are strong
> And you really do have worth ...

I ask the men to write about talents they have. If they wrote to themselves from the future, can they describe the life they have in this imaginary future and have always wanted to live? But none of the men are inspired, so I ask them to write about a good friend or relative, someone they love and why.

Both Curtis and Owen write about how much they love their mothers. Curtis says his mother is going to visit him on Saturday. He talks to her a lot on the phone. Owen says he doesn't want his mother to visit him, because he doesn't like to see her cry. But she is a wonderful mother. Sure, he would lie to her when he was young, and she would believe him. Like when someone told her he and his friend broke into the neighbour's house, which he did, but he said no, they were playing. But now he never lies to her.

I ask how mothers can create an atmosphere so their children are honest with them. I say, When mothers are honest with their sons, that helps. Yes, Owen agrees. The CO says, Teenagers don't tell their parents everything. I lied to my parents when I was a teenager.

Lynton writes about his stepfather, how good he was to Lynton, how he would listen to him, take him out for drives, take him to basketball practice.

I say, Parents are so important to kids. It doesn't have to be a biological parent. I say that the man I am married to now is not the biological father of my sons, but they are close to him. When they were growing up, my eldest son asked, "Do you think of us as your sons?" Parental figures have a big impact on families.

I say I would like my sons to write about me the way the men in this group write about their mothers. What should our actions be so we are parents our children love?

Then I ask the men what they can do so they will not return to prison.

Lynton says he has to stay away from his old gang who do crack. Owen says he hasn't thought about it. He has years in prison to think about it.

Curtis says he has to stay away from guns. I ask if he used guns to break in and enter. He says, No. Then he says he killed his best friend at a party by accident. The friend was the godfather of his son. He doesn't want to have a gun anymore.

Killed his best friend? By accident?

Curtis says he wrote a rap poem about it; he brought it to the workshop. Can he read it?

We are all keen to hear Curtis. He reads his poem, which is rhythmic and intense and has a lot of heart.

CHAPTER THIRTEEN

When I'm asked what I learned from working in the prison, I'm hesitant to answer because any response seems obvious. I saw clearly how alike we all are, how lucky we are if our family has not been injured beyond repair by poverty, racism, abuse, institutional trauma; how much we need each other, how inequality, as well as a punitive prison system, hurts everyone. When society limits people's possibilities and offers a life, to some, that is so bleak, the chance they will end up in prison greatly increases. But we all know this.

Julia, a woman in one of the workshops, said to me, "Why don't you write about what you learned from us? That's your assignment." I learned that everyone has a story to tell, a powerful, moving story. And people care about these stories. But most will never be heard. I wanted these stories to be heard.

In Mary Shelley's *Frankenstein*, the Creature is kind when he is first created. But after continuous rejection, when he finally understands he will never be loved or find sympathy from anyone, he wants revenge. In the 1994 film based on Shelley's novel, the Creature says, "There is love in me the likes of which you've never seen. There is rage in me the likes of which should never escape. If I am not satisfied in the one, I will indulge the other." He knows that his actions are heinous but when he sees clearly that the world offers him nothing and nothing will change, his despair overrides his morality. He cries out, "I was benevolent and good; misery made me a fiend. Make me happy, and I shall again be virtuous."[102]

Despite the murders he commits, readers feel sympathy for him because his story is complex, his suffering enormous. Mary Shelley's book asks the question, Why does someone act monstrously? By revealing the deeply rooted causes of brutality, Mary Shelley forces us to question our own complicity. As rapper Kendrick Lamar says, "... when you experience things like that [police brutality and racism] personally and you know the type of hardships and pain that it brings first-hand, it builds a certain rage in you."[103]

From Mary Shelley to Kendrick Lamar, the accusations are clear: Society's failure is our failure. Of course, most of the men and women in the prison where I worked did not commit murder. Several were on remand for offenses such as violating probation or trafficking marijuana.

I have been asked if my experience working with men and women differed. I observed striking differences. Men were generally more confident. If I asked a question about a poem we were reading in the men's workshop, participants responded with insightful interpretations. They were willing to risk being wrong. In the women's workshops, however, a common reply was, "I don't know. I don't understand poetry." But often, by the end of a discussion, these women revealed a profound comprehension and appreciation for the poem.

Women felt more shame about being in jail than men, in my observation. Often I'd think, "These women have no one to fight for them." This was not always the case, of course. But many of the women were so beaten down. Implicitly, they were held to a different standard than men and no matter how smart, talented, and compassionate they were, the unspoken word was that if you were a woman in prison you'd sunk to the bottom.

This was not true in the men's sections. For some, prison seemed like a rite of passage. Perhaps because for a man, a certain amount of violence is seen as acceptable in order to defend one's family and property. The men were not happy to be in prison, but they did not feel solely responsible for their fate. Several had relatives who were currently, or had been, in prison so incarceration did not appear to be so alien.

Quite a few male prisoners talked lovingly about their mothers and the sustenance they got from their families. Few women I worked with spoke about support they received from men in their lives, though some did. Many did not have support from women family members either. In additional to societal judgement, many women suffered the trauma of having their children taken from them or feared their children would be taken.

Gender hierarchy is complicated and I don't claim to have answers. But can people still question whether gender inequality exists? And how many studies do we need to show that growing up in poverty, in a segregated community, where funding for schools is lacking and illiteracy common, are factors that greatly increase the chances of incarceration? In wealthy neighbourhoods, where children have resources and are encouraged and supported to continue their education, the incarceration rate is ... take a guess.

When I am asked if the writing workshops were successful, if analyzing poetry and sharing writing assignments helped these men and women clarify their thinking and therefore their actions, all I can say is I hope so. But I am not the one to answer that question. Only the participants in the workshops have that answer.

I recently read a quote in "Word A Day" from the pastor John Hall, who died in 1898: "Kind words, kind looks, kind acts, and warm hand-shakes, these are means of grace when men in trouble are fighting their unseen battles." It gave me great pleasure to tell a participant in my workshop, "What you just read is terrific. Thank you for sharing this," and sincerely mean these words. Men and women in prison get so little positive feedback. I wanted to be an encouraging voice. Yet my workshops only lasted six weeks. And there were so few programs to encourage these gifted, creative, intelligent people.

The majority of participants were supportive of each other and enthusiastic about discussing poems. They expressed their appreciation that I was there. I am grateful they welcomed me into their space and trusted me. I don't take their trust lightly; it was a great gift to receive. The respect I felt for participants made the workshops, for me, moving and rewarding, but also distressing. After a year of volunteering in the prison, I was worn down.

I would come home from each session, write down what happened during the time I was there, eat a quick dinner, then go right to bed, drained. I saw, during each encounter, what pain these men and women carried, as well as the talent and intelligence that was not being nurtured. Though the connection I felt to participants was strong, as was my joy when I observed how proud they were to share their stories, my frustration and helplessness about their situation was overwhelming. And if I felt this way, imagine the despair and hopelessness incarcerated men and women feel.

Since I stopped working with men and women in the prison, I feel an absence. One goal I have is to give workshops for people outside prison suffering from post traumatic stress disorder, perhaps in conjunction with a therapeutic community. It is my experience that when people are offered a safe environment where they feel comfortable to write about any experience and share what they've written, they no longer feel isolated. Encouraging people to write is one way of letting them know their experiences are important; they are not alone.

CHAPTER FOURTEEN

I am in Vancouver writing these chapters. It is Valentine's Day and I go to a Qigong class that starts at six. But it takes a long time to get there, especially at this time of day, so I board the bus at about 3:15.

I went to Qigong class last week and it energized me. In one set of exercises we pounded the inside of our arms, continued up over our shoulders, then down the outside of our arms, past the elbows to the back of our hands. The instructor said pounding opens Qi energy.

As the bus moves toward downtown Vancouver, it takes on passengers at each stop and soon there are no more seats. At one of the stops people are lining up to get on the bus, but there is not enough room to accommodate more than one or two people. I am sitting by a window and when I look out I see a man, perhaps in his mid-forties, with long black hair down his back. He is a handsome man, tall and slim, with tanned, leathery skin. He is holding on to a walker. I smile at him. He smiles back. Then he sits on his walker. He is tired. The day is grey. He will not be getting on this bus. He is a young man, and to me mid-forties is young, sitting on a walker. I smile again and he smiles. Then he takes his fist and gently pounds his heart. I feel as if I am going to cry. It is as if he is saying, "I see you recognize that

I am a person, a man, a beautiful man; you do not just look through me, though you are comfortable, a woman with a 'seat on the bus.'" I take my fist and pound my heart too. He blows me a kiss. Then the bus starts moving.

POEMS

Poems we have been given permission to reproduce, in the order they were mentioned in chapters.

To My Room by Robert Berold

When I moved here you were much darker,
so I put in windows and the aerial bookshelf
that runs around above head height. Now
I sleep with a weight of books above my head.
I want to cover them, like birds, to keep them quiet.

I've slept three thousand nights in your arms.
You have absorbed my snoring and my dreams.
Your walls have seen dogs, spiders, frogs, a snake or
        two,
and once a porcupine ambled through.

The trees are coming into leaf today.
I tell you this slowly because you've never been
        outside.

(Berold, Robert. *All the Days*. Grahamstown, South Africa:
Deep South Books, 2008.)

Flower Shop by Jason Heroux

An old woman
pushing a stroller
paused in front
of a flower shop.
She stood on her
own dark shadow
as if it was a bridge
she was afraid to cross.
I'm not sure what
went through her mind.
She put on her gloves,
a chill was in the air,
and continued on her way.
All this happened years ago.
The flower shop is now torn
down and the woman is gone.
I watched her disappear around
the corner and then closed my eyes.
I'm not sure what went through my mind.

(Heroux, Jason. *Emergency Hallelujah*. Toronto, ON:
Mansfield Press, 2008.)

My Father's Love Letters by Yusef Komunyakaa

On Fridays he'd open a can of Jax
After coming home from the mill,
& ask me to write a letter to my mother
Who sent postcards of desert flowers
Taller than men. He would beg,
Promising to never beat her
Again. Somehow I was happy
She had gone, & sometimes wanted
To slip in a reminder, how Mary Lou
Williams' "Polka Dots & Moonbeams"
Never made the swelling go down.
His carpenter's apron always bulged
With old nails, a claw hammer
Looped at his side & extension cords
Coiled around his feet.
Words rolled from under the pressure
Of my ballpoint: Love,
Baby, Honey, Please.
We sat in the quiet brutality
Of voltage meters & pipe threaders,
Lost between sentences ...
The gleam of a five-pound wedge
On the concrete floor
Pulled a sunset
Through the doorway of his toolshed.
I wondered if she laughed
& held them over a gas burner.
My father could only sign
His name, but he'd look at blueprints
& say how many bricks
Formed each wall. This man,

Who stole roses & hyacinth
For his yard, would stand there
With eyes closed & fists balled,
Laboring over a simple word, almost
Redeemed by what he tried to say.

Two Songs by Campbell McGrath

Two Songs

1. North Carolina

The more you allow the figures of black, silent trees
glimpsed by night from the window of a train near
Fayetteville into your heart, the greater the burden
      you
must carry with you on your journey, and the sooner
you will come to question your ability to endure it,
and the stronger your conviction to sing.

2. Tiger

A tiger on our block, a real tiger, ivory and mallow
      orange,
coiled and sinewed, caged in the back of a pickup
      truck
in the driveway of the house of the two married
      models who
live three doors down, for a fashion shoot. These
      things happen
in Miami Beach. Beautiful, they are, beautiful animals.
Six months later she leaves him. And the sound of
      his rock and
roll band now, in the empty house, at all hours,
      practicing.

("Two Songs" from *Pax Atomica* by Campbell McGrath.
Copyright © 2004 by Campbell McGrath. Courtesy of
ECCO, an imprint of HarperCollins Publishers.)

The Trick by Julie Bruck

Blinking in the half-light, almost bright
after the school's dim corridors, we'd pass
the line of poplars, tall black sentries
at the outer limits of the play field.
Street lights flicked on, one at a time,
new snow coming down, heavy and wet.
We ran the hill and slid, our boots
etching serpentines on the snowy sidewalk.
A big boulevard to cross, then the empty
lot, whose Scotch pines knelt beneath
the snow's accumulation, blue in this light,
before the final, dangerous curve.
We always sensed them, were never
prepared for the three or four boys
crouched between the blind flanks
of houses, coiled to grab our hats and run
with impossible suddenness, schoolbags slung
like ammo belts across their eight-year-old chests.
We jammed the hats our mothers bought
deep in our pockets like charms – anything
to deflect their rough attentions,
though I knew it meant they liked us:
I had two brothers and understood
to love meant to torment.
A schoolmate's mother, who sang
in a barbershop quartet,
had already hung herself at home.
Another child's father would soon seal
his garage door with duct tape,
and start the family car.
She left no note, his would say,

he loved them all. I thought the trick
was to sidestep even the smallest emergencies,
disappear in our blue or grey duffel coats,
hats clamped in our wet fists, to will
them by like fire engines when the fire
is elsewhere and much more urgent – until
they'd blown past, their boisterous voices
receding, and three or four Canadiens jackets
drew so close to the vanishing point,
you could hide them by holding up a thumb.
We'd walk home quietly in the softly
falling snow, small monks who remained,
to all appearances, untouched.

(Bruck, Julie. *Monkey Ranch*. London, ON: Brick Books, 2012.)

What I Hated by Robert Berold

what I hated
was the way they used to laugh

the way pain and confusion
was funny to them

the way they would ask questions
and laugh at your answer

what are you looking at? nothing
you call me nothing?

the way they spoke about beating up kaffirs
what had kaffirs ever done to them or me?

the way I was torn between wanting to be part of
    them
and wanting nothing to do with them

and if I wasn't part of them
what was I part of?

(Berold, Robert. *All The Days*. Grahamstown, South Africa:
Deep South Books, 2008.)

Call Me By My True Names by Thich Nhat Hanh

Do not say that I'll depart tomorrow
because even today I still arrive.

Look deeply: I arrive in every second
to be a bud on a spring branch,
to be a tiny bird, with wings still fragile,
learning to sing in my new nest,
to be a caterpillar in the heart of a flower,
to be a jewel hiding itself in a stone.

I still arrive, in order to laugh and to cry,
in order to fear and to hope.
The rhythm of my heart is the birth and
death of all that are alive.

I am the mayfly metamorphosing on the surface of
        the river,
and I am the bird which, when spring comes, arrives
    · in time
to eat the mayfly.

I am the frog swimming happily in the clear pond,
and I am also the grass-snake who, approaching in
        silence,
feeds itself on the frog.

I am the child in Uganda, all skin and bones,
my legs as thin as bamboo sticks,
and I am the arms merchant, selling deadly weapons
        to Uganda.

I am the twelve-year-old girl, refugee on a small boat,
who throws herself into the ocean after being raped
    by a sea pirate,
and I am the pirate, my heart not yet capable of
    seeing and loving.

I am a member of the politburo, with plenty of
    power in my hands,
and I am the man who has to pay his "debt of blood"
    to my people,
dying slowly in a forced labor camp.

My joy is like spring, so warm it makes flowers
    bloom in all walks of life.
My pain if like a river of tears, so full it fills the four
    oceans.

Please call me by my true names,
so I can hear all my cries and laughs at once,
so I can see that my joy and pain are one.

Please call me by my true names,
so I can wake up,
and so the door of my heart can be left open,
the door of compassion.

(Thich Nhat Hanh. *Call Me By My True Names: The Collected Poems of Thich Nhat Hanh.* Berkeley, CA: Parallax Press, 1999.)

The Old Man by Carole Glasser Langille

When I die the old man who lives inside me
will give me his blessing
and tend my body.

I forced him to lie shivering
in cold water
and he forgave me.

Eyes lively, he will oil my feet,
smooth my hands.
Each moment I approach death

he grows younger, stronger.
"There's so much I wanted,"
I tell him. *Soon*, he says

you will want nothing. When I die
the old man who lives inside me
will be ready and willing with answers.

Though I, deep in his body
will need no answers.
I'll have no questions.

(Langille, Carole Glasser. *Church of the Exquisite Panic: The Ophelia Poems*. St. John's, NL: Pedlar Press, 2012.)

Cock by Carole Glasser Langille

You strutted like a cock while I was doomed
to walk at dusk among trees,
my thoughts burning, and still
I could not find
my way. As if night were unconscious,
I went through its pockets: dry white sand
and cockle shells, luminous, reflecting moons.
Oh but they were funny,
the snatches of song I heard. *For some must watch
and some must wait.* I walked
till the first cock crowed, cockeyed,
dreaming I would find you in your boat,
unmoored, remembering
how you fell to such a study of my face. My brother
     was wrong,
your words gave more heat than light.
Let me say it again: Cock of the walk,
cock of the rock, cocksure,
the morning is cockshy, struggling to rid itself
of dream. By what shift did you decide to hold,
not me, but that which
would forever be withheld?
You brushed against me
even as you turned. Man who ate air,
here I am with your words
in my mouth, tongue-tied.
I would not have thought love could survive
so much scorn and sorrow.

(Langille, Carole Glasser. *Church of the Exquisite Panic: The Ophelia Poems.* St. John's, NL: Pedlar Press, 2012.)

Pricked by John Terpstra

I have fallen in love with yet another woman.
Is she beautiful? I do not know. I cannot be objective.
She is not a Shih Tzu or a pug,
if that's what you're asking.

The longer she spoke the stronger the attraction grew.
She pointed out adverse reactions
some people have (very few, it turns out),
and I wondered what were the odds

that I was one of those few, or that such a woman
would fall in love with me.
I was conscious of my age, to tell the truth.
She was not too young. Would she be immune?

She touched my arm lightly
just above the elbow, and laughed.
What we were talking about,
I forgot.

Funny, isn't it? I am willing to fall in love
with almost any woman that I meet,
(some more willingly than others)
as readily as others catch cold or the flu.

The woman who works as a labourer
at a construction site up the street.
The last time I drove past,
she was loading bricks into a wheelbarrow.

Even the women sitting in a quiet row
under the dark windows, waiting their turn
for inoculation, and old enough to be my mother –
a scary thought.

The woman I fell in love with last night
had been easing apprehensions all evening.
When she reached to prick a needle into my arm
she had so recently touched, I felt nothing.

(Terpstra, John. *Brilliant Falls*. Kentville, NS: Gaspereau Press, 2013.)

Too Late by Carole Glasser Langille

Already it is too late
to start over. So many people
I'll never be, things I won't do.
Why list them? Soon the years ahead
will be too few to maneuver among
and I won't be able to lie, even to myself.
As in a cave at low tide, echoes resound,
not in the spaciousness of possibility,
but in limitation. And isn't this good?
To say, *"Yes, I haven't. That's right, I never did."*

(Langille, Carole Glasser. *Late in a Slow Time*. Toronto, ON: Mansfield Press, 2003.)

What Saves Us by Bruce Weigl

We are wrapped around each other in
the back of my father's car parked
in the empty lot of the high school
of our failures, the sweat on her neck
like oil. The next morning I would leave
for the war and I thought I had something
coming for that, I thought to myself
that I would not die never having
been inside her long body. I pulled
her skirt above her waist like an umbrella
blown inside out by the storm. I pulled
her cotton panties up as high as
she could stand. I was on fire. Heaven
was in sight. We were drowning on our
tongues and I tried to tear my pants off
when she stopped so suddenly
we were surrounded only by my shuddering
and by the school bells grinding in the
empty halls. She reached to find something,
a silver crucifix on a silver
chain, the tiny savior's head hanging
and stakes through his hands and his feet.
She put it around my neck and held
me so long the black wings of my heart
were calmed. We are not always right
about what we think will save us.
I thought that dragging the angel down would
save me, but instead I carried the crucifix
in my pocket and rubbed it on my
face and lips nights the rockets roared in.

People die sometimes so near you
you feel them struggling to cross over,
the deep untangling, of one body from another.

(Weigl, Bruce. *What Saves Us*. Evanston, IL: Northwestern
University Press, 1992.)

Desiderata by Max Ehrmann

Go placidly amid the noise and haste,
and remember what peace there may be in silence.
As far as possible without surrender
be on good terms with all persons.
Speak your truth quietly and clearly;
and listen to others,
even the dull and the ignorant;
they too have their story.

Avoid loud and aggressive persons,
they are vexations to the spirit.
If you compare yourself with others,
you may become vain and bitter;
for always there will be greater and lesser persons
    than yourself.
Enjoy your achievements as well as your plans.

Keep interested in your own career, however humble;
it is a real possession in the changing fortunes of
    time.
Exercise caution in your business affairs;
for the world is full of trickery.
But let this not blind you to what virtue there is;
many persons strive for high ideals;
and everywhere life is full of heroism.

222 – Carole Glasser Langille

Be yourself.
Especially, do not feign affection.
Neither be cynical about love;
for in the face of all aridity and disenchantment
it is as perennial as the grass.

Take kindly the counsel of the years,
gracefully surrendering the things of youth.
Nurture strength of spirit to shield you in sudden
    misfortune.
But do not distress yourself with dark imaginings.
Many fears are born of fatigue and loneliness.
Beyond a wholesome discipline,
be gentle with yourself.

You are a child of the universe,
no less than the trees and the stars;
you have a right to be here.
And whether or not it is clear to you,
no doubt the universe is unfolding as it should.

Therefore be at peace with God,
whatever you conceive Him to be,
and whatever your labors and aspirations,
in the noisy confusion of life keep peace with your
    soul.

With all its sham, drudgery, and broken dreams,
it is still a beautiful world.
Be cheerful.
Strive to be happy.

(Max Ehrmann, "Desiderata." maxehrmann.com)

Not in the Warm Earth by Carole Glasser Langille

This is where we come
to find our parents.
In the fine cloth. In the neat hand. Did you
make this for me, mother? Are you
proud, father? Though I didn't
hit the ball, though I didn't
go to meetings.

I lived mostly in my dreams. Remember,
I would go into the yard, my bike
a horse. I'd race. I'd vault
fences. By the time I got home,
I'd crossed the border,
was in my late thirties, children
holding both my hands.
New lock on an old door.

This is where we find our parents,
white water rafting down rapids
in the same boat we're in.
But it tips, it turns over.
I can't save them.

In the middle of the night
they wake me. They tell me I've made mistake
after mistake. They're worried.
I get up. Heat milk. Tell them
I visit often. Am still touched
by incandescent moments
of their great caring, their heroic endeavours.
I know how hard it was to live
in that house. In that life.

"But, mother, it's late. Father, you're dead, it's time
you were asleep. When you *do* visit
you don't have to rattle the doors.
Knock gently, I'll be listening. Tell me
why you have come. What can I give you?

(Langille, Carole Glasser. *Late in a Slow Time*. Toronto,
ON: Mansfield Press, 2003.)

Ithaka by Constantine Cavafy

As you set out for Ithaka
hope your road is a long one,
full of adventure, full of discovery.
Laistrygonians, Cyclops,
angry Poseidon – don't be afraid of them:
you'll never find things like that on your way
as long as you keep your thoughts raised high,
as long as a rare excitement
stirs your spirit and your body.
Laistrygonians, Cyclops,
wild Poseidon – you won't encounter them
unless you bring them along inside your soul,
unless your soul sets them up in front of you.

Hope your road is a long one.
May there be many summer mornings when,
with what pleasure, what joy,
you enter harbors you're seeing for the first time;
may you stop at Phoenician trading stations
to buy fine things,
mother of pearl and coral, amber and ebony,
sensual perfume of every kind –

as many sensual perfumes as you can;
and may you visit many Egyptian cities
to learn and go on learning from their scholars.

Keep Ithaka always in your mind.
Arriving there is what you're destined for.
But don't hurry the journey at all.
Better if it lasts for years,
so you're old by the time you reach the island,
wealthy with all you've gained on the way,
not expecting Ithaka to make you rich.

Ithaka gave you the marvelous journey.
Without her you wouldn't have set out.
She has nothing left to give you now.

And if you find her poor, Ithaka won't have fooled
     you.
Wise as you will have become, so full of experience,
you'll have understood by then what these Ithakas
     mean.

(C.P. Cavafy, "Ithaka" from *C.P. Cavafy: Collected Poems*
Princeton, NJ: Princeton University Press, 1975. Translated
by Edmund Keeley and Philip Sherrard. Translation
Copyright © 1975, 1992 by Edmund Keeley and Philip
Sherrard.)

Loving, Writing by Tom Pow

If your love was true
and you lose it, what have you lost?
Not the act of loving. That's yours.

If your words were true
and you lose them, what have you lost?
Not the act of writing. That's yours too.

In loving, in writing, how can you
hold onto a finished thing? Whether
you lose it or put it beneath glass,

it is the act itself you must cherish.
For what's left when the moment has passed,
the wind will carry. Despite you.

(Pow, Tom. *Red Letter Day*. Hexham, UK: Bloodaxe Books, 1996.)

Sleep Chains by Anne Carson

Who can sleep when she –
hundreds of miles away I feel that vast breath
fan her restless decks.
Cicatrice by cicatrice
all the links
rattle once.
Here we go mother on the shipless ocean.
Pity us, pity the ocean, here we go.

(Carson, Anne. *Decreation*. Toronto, ON: Vintage Canada, 2005.)

Kimberly Rogers by Carole Glasser Langille

You won't be there to greet her,
a woman alone and so big.
You will lose sight of her,
eight months pregnant in a bare
apartment. You will not be able to find her,
under house arrest, refrigerator

empty. She had undeclared student loans,
a judge who passed sentence: *You lied
and stole from your community.*
She had a mother she'd just reconciled with,
a government that cut off benefits, drugs
from her doctor.

You will not be the one to find
her decomposing body in the sweltering
apartment. Go meet her.
She is still in her room
where she made preparations. See how the baby
lies still in her belly,

how the body stays put
in the place it's assigned.
Just do not ask her
to get up and start over.

(Langille, Carole Glasser. *Church of the Exquisite Panic: The Ophelia Poems.* St. John's, NL: Pedlar Press, 2012.)

The Hour is Turning by Rainer Maria Rilke
Da neigt sich die Stunde und rührt mich an

The hour is striking so close above me,
so clear and sharp,
that all my senses ring with it.
I feel it now: there's a power in me
to grasp and give shape to my world.

I know that nothing has ever been real
without my beholding it.
All becoming has needed me.
My looking ripens things
and they come toward me, to meet and be met.

(Rilke, Rainer Maria. *Rilke's Book of Hours: Love Poems to God*. Translated by Anita Barrows and Joanna Macy. New York, NY: Riverhead, 1996.)

When Leather is a Whip by Martín Espada

At night,
with my wife
sitting on the bed,
I turn from her
to unbuckle
my belt
so she won't see
her father
unbuckling
his belt

(Espada, Martín. *Alabanza: New and Selected Poems 1982-2002*. New York, NY: W.W. Norton & Co., 2004.)

Has My Heart Gone To Sleep by Antonio Machado

Has my heart gone to sleep?
Have the beehives of my dreams
stopped working, the waterwheel
of the mind run dry,
scoops turning empty,
only shadow inside?

No, my heart is not asleep.
It is awake, wide awake.
Not asleep, not dreaming –
its eyes are opened wide
watching distant signals, listening
on the rim of vast silence.

(https://www.poemhunter.com/poem/has-my-heart-gone-to-sleep/)

Acquainted with the Night by Robert Frost

I have been one acquainted with the night.
I have walked out in rain – and back in rain.
I have outwalked the furthest city light.

I have looked down the saddest city lane.
I have passed by the watchman on his beat
And dropped my eyes, unwilling to explain.

I have stood still and stopped the sound of feet
When far away an interrupted cry
Came over houses from another street,

But not to call me back or say good-bye;
And further still at an unearthly height,
One luminary clock against the sky

Proclaimed the time was neither wrong nor right.
I have been one acquainted with the night.

(Frost, Robert. *The Poetry of Robert Frost. The collected
poems, complete and unabridged.* Edward Connery Lathem,
ed. Stamford, CT: Thomson Learning, 1969.)

A Dream Deferred by Langston Hughes

What happens to a dream deferred?
Does it dry up
Like a raisin in the sun?
Or fester like a sore –
And then run?
Does it stink like rotten meat?
Or crust and sugar over –
like a syrupy sweet?
Maybe it just sags
like a heavy load.
Or does it explode?

(Hughes, Langston. *The Collected Poems of Langston Hughes*. New York, NY: Vintage, 1995.)

234 - Carole Glasser Langille

Left by Carole Glasser Langille

My old dog hauls herself awake to follow
    up and down stairs when I get chocolate,
a ripe plum, stays close as I read
    a letter about Michael, boy I met at camp
when I was fifteen. He was sick as a dog
    that summer, hospitals, colostomy. But he calmed
us all with his heart-to-hearts. Mine I hid,
    mostly from myself. When we kissed
I thought, *here's a place to be admitted*. For a time,
    when I pressed against railings, I believed
I was separate from what lay beyond. The body
    is an alibi when the mind roams. Years later,
he waited hours in a blizzard for my plane
    when I visited. We both had children then.

    I don't know what followed him
up and down his own stairs,
    what his days were like before he died, paralyzed
in a hospice, his mind clear, his children young.
    The ripe plum of his kiss, echo of his laugh
like my dog running close
    then bounding away. This can't be
all that's left: a face that smiles and leans towards me
    and lingers, but has nothing more to say.

(Mooney, Jacob McArthur, Molly Peacock, and Anita Lahey, eds. *The Best Canadian Poetry in English 2015*. Toronto: ON: Tightrope Books Inc., 2015.)

On Attachment by Suzanne Buffam

A house burns all night.
In the middle of a field.
A beautiful sight
Even if the burning house
Does happen to be mine.
Sooner or later
All burning houses will be mine.

(Buffam, Suzanne. *The Irrationalist*. Toronto, ON: House of
Anansi Press, 2010.)

ICU by Spencer Reece
For A.J. Verdelle

Those mornings I traveled north on I91,
passing below the basalt cliff of East Rock
where the elms discussed their genealogies.
I was a chaplain at Hartford Hospital,
took the Myers-Briggs with Sister Margaret,
learned I was an *I* drawn to *Es*.
In small groups I said, "I do not like it –
the way so many young black men die here
unrecognized, their gurneys stripped,
their belongings catalogued and unclaimed."
On the neonatal ICU, newborns breathed,
blue, spider-delicate in a nest of tubes.
A Sunday of themselves, their tissue purpled,
their eyelids the film on old water in a well,
their faces resigned in their see-through attics,
their skin mottled mildewed wallpaper.
It is correct to love even at the wrong time.
On rounds, the newborns eyed me, each one
like Orpheus in his dark hallway, saying:
I knew I would find you, I knew I would lose you.

(Reece, Spencer. *The Road to Emmaus*. New York, NY:
Farrar, Straus and Giroux, 2015.)

ACKNOWLEDGEMENTS

I'm indebted to the poets who gave permission to reprint their work. Thank you.

Thank you, Mindy Lewis, exquisite writer, for your wonderful suggestions on many, many chapters.

Thank you to the wonderful Jan Barkhouse, Chris Benjamin, Marion Moore, for reading early chapters of this manuscript and giving terrific feedback. I am so lucky to call each of you friend.

Thank you, Marilyn Iwama, beautiful sister, for all your help.

Thank you, Lesley Carson, for formatting the manuscript, and making excellent suggestions. You have many talents.

Thank you, Mia, for allowing us to print your story "Scars."

Thank you, David Fleming, for letting me share the line you wrote as a student in my class at Dalhousie. Following the Pinsky line, "When I had / No lover I courted my sleep," you wrote, "And even sleep held out on me."

Thank you to my editor Julia Swan. Our email conversations about my experience in the prison led to further insights about the men and women I met there. And your suggestions were brilliant.

Thank you, Lesley Choyce. Your dedication to writers, your support, your courage, your kindness, mean everything.

Thanks to the Joy Kogawa House for the wonderful gift of being a writer-in-residence. I finished most of the manuscript during this time.

Thank you, Diana Rothenberg, Mara Goodman, Sally Hutchinson, Alex Thurman, Rita Glen, for your support and encouragement.

Thank you, Caleb Langille and Luke Langille, for your wisdom and for so many insights.

To Bill Hardstaff, many many thanks. Without you, how?

ENDNOTES

1. Salzman, Mark. *True Notebooks, A Writer's Year at Juvenile Hall.* New York, NY: Vintage Books, 2004.

2. Stevenson, Bryan S. *Just Mercy, A Story of Justice and Redemption.* New York, NY: Spiegel & Grau, 2014.

3. Quotes from Wallace Stevens and M.S. Merwin: Halperin, Daniel. "A Few Questions for Poetry." *The New York Times Book Review.* December 30, 2016.

4. http://www.statcan.gc.ca/pub/85-002-x/2016001/ article/14318-eng.htm

5. "How I Go To The Woods" by Mary Oliver. nature-poems. com/how-i-go-to-the-woods-nature.html

6. "To My Room" by Robert Berold. From *All the Days.* Grahamstown, South Africa: Deep South, 2008.

7. "Flower Shop" by Jason Heroux. From *Emergency Hallelujah.* Toronto, ON: Mansfield Press, 2008.

8. "My Father's Love Letters" from *Pleasure Dome: New and Collected Poems* © 2001 by Yusef Komunyakaa. Published by Wesleyan University Press and reprinted with permission.

9. "Two Songs" from *Pax Atomica* by Campbell McGrath. Copyright © 2004 by Campbell McGrath. Courtesy of ECCO, an imprint of HarperCollins Publishers.

10. Bessel van der Kolk: Information from Delancyplace.com from *The Body Keeps the Score* by Bessel van der Kolk, M.D. Date accessed July 31, 2019.

11. "The Trick" by Julie Bruck. From *Monkey Ranch*. London, ON: Brick Books, 2012.

12. "What I Hated" by Robert Berold. From *All the Days*. Grahamstown, South Africa: Deep South, 2008.

13. "Call Me By My True Names" by Thich Nhat Hanh. From *Call Me By My True Names: The Collected Poems of Thich Nhat Hanh.* Berkeley, CA: Parallax Press, 2001.

14. From Dr. Angela Davis's inaugural Viola Desmond Legacy Lecture and Belong Forum, October 16, 2018, as part of Dalhousie University's 200th anniversary celebrations. https://www.youtube.com/watch?v=IFM26MDyIU0

15. Preventions of Deaths in Custody from: "Conditions of Confinement." Government of Canada. Office of the Correctional Investigator (Howard Sapers). 2014-15 Annual Report, Backgrounder. https://www.oci-bec.gc.ca/cnt/comm/presentations/presentationsAR-RA1415info-eng.aspx Date accessed July 19, 2019

16. "Correctional Investigator Reflects on Key Challenges in his latest Annual Report to Parliament." Government of Canada. Office of the Office of the Correctional Investigator (Harold Sapers). 2014-15 Annual Report. https://www.oci-bec.gc.ca/cnt/comm/press/press20160310-eng.aspx Date accessed July 19, 2019

17. Line from "There Are Things I Tell To No One" by Galway Kinnell: *Mortal Acts. Mortal Words.* Boston, MA: Houghton Mifflin Harcourt, 1980. Line from "Heart" by Donald Justice: Donald Justice, *Selected Poems*, New York, NY: Atheneum, 1983. Line from "Impression" by Patrick Lane: *Selected Poems: 1977-1997*. Madeira Park, BC: Harbour Publishing, 1997. Line from "Crossings" by Alison Smith: *The*

Wedding House. Kentville, NS: Gaspereau Press, 2000. Line from "A Moment of Pure Waking" by A. F. Moritz: *Rest on the Flight into Egypt*. London, ON: Brick Books, 1999. Line adapted from "Blossoms" by Harry Thurston: *Keeping Watch at the End of the World*. Kentville, NS: Gaspereau Press, 2005.

18. "Dedication" by Czeslaw Milosz. From *The Collected Poems: 1931-1987*. Copyright © 1988 by Czeslaw Milosz Royalties, Inc. Used by permission of HarperCollins Publishers.

19. "Love" by Czeslaw Milosz. From *The Collected Poems: 1931-1987*. Copyright © 1988 by Czeslaw Milosz Royalties, Inc. Used by permission of HarperCollins Publishers.

20. "The Old Man" by Carole Glasser Langille. From *Church of the Exquisite Panic: The Ophelia Poems*. St. John's, NL: Pedlar Press, 2012.

21. "Cock" by Carole Glasser Langille. From *Church of the Exquisite Panic: The Ophelia Poems*. St. John's, NL: Pedlar Press, 2012.

22. "Too Late" by Carole Glasser Langille. From *Late In A Slow Time*. Toronto, ON: Mansfield Press, 2003.

23. "The Gift" by Li-Young Lee. From *Rose*. Rochester, NY: BOA Editions Ltd., 1986.

24 "Pricked" by John Terpstra. From *Brilliant Falls*. Kentville, NS: Gaspereau Press, 2013.

25. Lines from "Exposure" by Robin Robertson. From www.poetryfoundation.org. Source: *Poetry* April 2002. Page 15. https://www.poetryfoundation.org/poetrymagazine/issue/71381/april-2002#toc

26. "Happiness" by Raymond Carver. From *All of Us: The Collected Poems*. New York, NY: Vintage, 2000.

27. Lines from Thich Nhat Hanh https://hackspirit.com/
25-profound-quotes-thich-nhat-hanh-will-make-rethink-love-
life-happiness/; and hackspirit.com/25-quotes-famous-
buddhist-master-will-make-rethink-life-live-happiness-1

28. Information on solitary confinement
https://www.vice.com/en_ca/article/
why-canadas- prisons-abuse-solitary-confinement

29. "Looking At Them Asleep" by Sharon Olds. From *The
Matter of This World*. Nottingham, UK: Slow Dancer Press,
1987.

30. "What Saves Us" by Bruce Weigl. From *What Saves Us*.
Evanston, IN: Northwestern University Press, 1992.

31. From Dr. Erin Wunker's talk at the Halifax, Nova Scotia,
march to support the Women's March on Washington,
January 21, 2017. She is an Assistant Professor in the English
Department at Dalhousie University.

32. "Desiderata" by Max Ehrmann mwkworks.com/desiderata.
html

33. "Quickthorn" by Siobhán Campbell. From www.
poetryfoundation.org Source: *Poetry*. December 2007. Page
206. https://www.poetryfoundation.org/poetrymagazine/
browse?contentId=49977

34. Got Your Back from July 25, 2014. *This American Life*.
Host Ira Glass. https://www.thisamericanlife.org

35. "Not in the Warm Earth" by Carole Glasser Langille. From
Late in a Slow Time. Toronto, ON: Mansfield Press, 2003.

36. Mann, Thomas. *Essays of Three Decades*. London, UK:
Secker & Warburg, 1947.

37. Rumi quotes: http://wisdomquotes.com/rumi-quotes/ Date
accessed June 3 2014.

38. John Edgar Wideman, "Newborn Thrown in Trash and Dies." *All Stories Are True*. New York, NY: Vintage, 1993.

39. Aileen Donnelly. "More than half of Canadian adults in jail awaiting trial rather than serving sentences in 2014 and 2015: StatsCan." *National Post* January 11, 2017. https://nationalpost.com/news/canada/more-than-half-of-canadian-adults-in-jail-awaiting-trial-rather-than-serving-sentences-in-2014-and-2015-statscan Date accessed July 22, 2019.

40. McGregor, Phlis and Angela MacIvor. "Black people 3 times more likely to be street checked in Halifax, police say." CBC Investigates. January 9, 2017. https://www.cbc.ca/news/canada/nova-scotia/halifax-black-street-checks-police-race-profiling-1.3925251 Date accessed: July 19, 2019. "Black people in Halifax 6 times more likely to be street checked than whites." CBC News. March 27, 2019. https://www.cbc.ca/news/canada/nova-scotia/street-checks-halifax-police-scot-wortley-racial-profiling-1.5073300 Date accessed July 19, 2019.

41. Eleanor Fischer's 1962 interview with Dr. Martin Luther King, Jr. https://www.wnyc.org/story/261384-previously-unreleased-interviews-reverend-dr-martin-luther-king-jr/ and https://www.gpbnews.org/post/rare-martin-luther-king-jr-interview-uncovered. Eleanor Fischer (1935-2008) began producing documentaries for the Canadian Broadcasting Corporation in the 1960s. She founded the New York office of National Public Radio and produced documentaries on Paul Robeson, Robert Frost, Martin Luther King, Jr., and Malcolm X, among others.

42. https://www.nytimes.com/2017/01/27/opinion/sunday/why-succeeding-against-the-odds-can-make-you-sick.html

43. Doucette, Keith. "Nova Scotia human rights board awards nearly $600,000 for racist discrimination." The Canadian Press. Global News. May 15, 2019. https://globalnews.ca/news/5278956/human-rights-board-600000-for-racist-discrimination/ Date accessed August 6, 2019.

44. Yeats, William Butler. *The Celtic Twilight.* https://archive.org/details/celtictwilight00yeatrich/page/n12; also https://polyarchive.com/william-butler-yeats-on-poetry/

45. "The Legend" by Garrett Hongo. From *The River of Heaven.* Pittsburgh, PA: Carnegie Mellon University Press, 2001.

46. Eckhart Tolle. *The Power of One: A Guide to Spiritual Enlightenment.* Audiobook. Novato, CA: New World Library, 2000.

47. "Eating Together," "Eating Alone" by Li-Young Lee. From *Rose.* Rochester, NY: BOA Editions Ltd., 1986.

48. "Sounds" by Howard Altmann. From *In This House.* Brooklyn, NY: Turtle Point Press, 2010.

49. Quotes from Justice Minister Landry and provincial Progressive Conservative leader https://www.theglobeandmail.com/news/national/nova-scotia-government-extends-programs-that-pairs-prisoners-with-pound-puppies/article13304549/ Date accessed July 20 2015.

50 "Persimmons" by Li-Young Lee. From *Rose.* Rochester, NY: BOA Editions Ltd., 1986.

51 "Samurai Song" by Robert Pinsky. From *Jersey Rain.* New York, NY: Farrar, Straus and Giroux, 2000.

52. "On The Amtrak From Boston To New York City" by Sherman Alexie http://www.poemhunter.com/poem/on-the-amtrak-from-boston-to-new-york-city/June 8, 2009

53. "Don't Do That" by Stephen Dunn. From *Here and Now: Poems*. New York, NY: WW Norton, 2013.

54. Woodbury, Richard. "Nova Scotia Records 192% jump in inmates presumed innocent and awaiting trial." CBC News. January 12, 2017. https://www.cbc.ca/news/canada/nova-scotia/nova-scotia-inmates-statistics-canada-report-remand-1.3931582 Date accessed July 19, 2019. Luck, Shaina. CBC News. May 20, 2016. https://www.cbc.ca/news/canada/nova-scotia/black-indigenous-prisoners-nova-scotia-jails-1.3591535

55. https://www150.statcan.gc.ca/n1/pub/85-002-x/2016001/article/14318-eng.htm Date accessed July 23, 2019

56. "Ithaka" by Constantine Cavafy. From *C.P. Cavafy: Collected Poems*. Translated by Edmund Keeley and Philip Sherrard. Princeton, NJ: Princeton University Press, 1975. Translators Copyright © 1975, 1992 by Edmund Keeley and Philip Sherrard.

57. "The Poetry of C.P. Cavafy." E.M. Forster. Published in *Pharos and Pharillon*. Poetryfoundation.org/poets/c-p-cavafy

58. "On The Nature of Understanding" by Kay Ryan. From *The Best of It: New and Selected Poems*. New York, NY: Grove Press, 2010.

59. "Loving, Writing" by Tom Pow. From *Red Letter Day*. Hexham, UK: Bloodaxe Books, 1996.

60. "Sleep Chains" by Anne Carson. From *Decreation*. Toronto, ON: Vintage Canada, 2005.

61. "Not Waving but Drowning" by Stevie Smith. From *New Selected Poems*. New York: NY: New Directions Publishing Corporation, 1988. https://www.poetryfoundation.org/poems/46479/not-waving-but-drowning)

62. "At the Wellhead" by Seamus Heaney. https://www.newyorker.com/magazine/1994/03/28/at-the-wellhead

63. "Power" by Adrienne Rich. https://allpoetry.com/poem/11641436-Power-by-Adrienne-Rich; https://www.best-poems.net/adrienne_rich/power.html

64. "Kimberly Rogers" by Carole Glasser Langille. From *Church of the Exquisite Panic: The Ophelia Poems*. St. John's, NL: Pedlar Press, 2012.

65. https://www.ccja-acjp.ca/pub/en/news/correctional-investigator-reflects/ Date accessed: March 1, 2017.

66. Statistics from: Why are Indigenous women disproportionately represented in federal prisons? https://www.cbc.ca/radio/thecurrent/the-current-for-march-28-2018-1.4595735/why-are-indigenous-women-disproportionately-represented-in-federal-prisons-1.\ Also https://www.oci-bec.gc.ca/cnt/rpt/annrpt/ann-rpt20142015-eng.aspx#s8

67. From an article by Chantelle Bellrichard, CBC News https://newsinteractives.cbc.ca/longform/locked-up-at-12 Date accessed August 3, 2019.

68. *Tower*. Podcast on *Fresh Air* on NPR. February 14, 2017. https://www.npr.org/2017/02/08/514001421/tower-pays-tribute-to-a-1966-campus-shooting-that-was-pushed-aside Date accessed February 18, 2017. *Tower*. Director Keith Maitland. Kino Lorber. 2016. Film.

69. Rumi quotes: http://wisdomquotes.com/rumi-quotes/ Date accessed June 3, 2014.

70. "Beauty" by Tony Hoagland. From *Donkey Gospel*. St. Paul, MN: Graywolf Press, 1998.

71. https://www.cbc.ca/news/canada/nova-scotia/clayton-cromwell-burnside-jail-death-inmate-1.4862493 in an article entitled "Intercom found to have been intentionally disabled

in Burnside jail death." Michael Tutton. The Canadian Press. October 14, 2018. https://www.theglobeandmail.com/canada/article-emergency-intercom-had-been-disabled-in-cell-of-halifax-man-who died/

72. https://www.cbc.ca/news/canada/nova-scotia/methadone-nova-scotia-jail-burnside-clayton-cromwell-1.3836706 in an article entitled "Clayton Cromwell's death prompts stricter methadone policies in jail." Angela McIvor. CBC News. November 7, 2016.

73. Rilke quote from Rilke's *Book of Hours, Love Poems to God*, translated by Anita Barrows and Joanna Macy. New York, NY: Riverhead Books, 1996.

74. "When Leather is a Whip" by Martín Espada. From *Alabanza: New and Selected Poems 1982-2002*. New York, NY: W.W. Norton & Company, 2004.

75. https://sites.northwestern.edu/jac8008/2014/05/16/czeslaw-milosz-a-story/

76. "Call Me By My True Names," by Thich Nhat Hanh. From *Call Me By My True Names: The Collected Poems of Thich Nhat Hanh*. Berkeley, CA: Parallax Press, 2001.

77. https://www.nytimes.com/2015/06/22/magazine/the-condition-of-black-life-is-one-of-mourning.html

78. Segal, Senator Hugh. "Tough on poverty, tough on crime." *The Star*. February 20, 2011. https://www.thestar.com/opinion/editorialopinion/2011/02/20/tough_on_poverty_tough_on_crime.html Date accessed July 24, 2019.

79. Reitano, Julie. "Adult correctional statistics in Canada, 2014/2015." Statistics Canada. https://www150.statcan.gc.ca/n1/pub/85-002-x/2016001/article/14318-eng.html Date accessed July 24, 2019.

80 "Her Kind" by Anne Sexton. From *The Complete Poems: Anne Sexton*. Boston, MA: Houghton Mifflin, 1981.

81. "Her Kind" by Carole Glasser Langille. From *In Cannon Cave*. London, ON: Brick Books, 1997.

82. Thank you, Liane Heller for your advice.

83. https://www.poemhunter.com/has-my-heart-gone-to-sleep

84. https://cbc.ca/radio/podcastplaylist/episode-3-tell-me-a-story-1.3135953

85. Government of Canada. Office of the Correctional Investigator (Howard Sapers), 2014-15 Annual Report, Backgrounder. https://www.oci-bec.gc.ca/cnt/comm/presentations/presentationsAR-RA1415info-eng.aspx Date accessed July 25, 2019.

86. "Aquainted With The Night" by Robert Frost. From *The Poetry of Robert Frost*, edited by Edward Connery Lathem. New York, NY: Henry Holt & Company, 1964, 1970. https://poetryfoundation.prg/poems/47548/acquainted-with-the-night

87. "A Dream Deferred" by Langston Hughes. From *The Collected Poems of Langston Hughes*. New York, NY: Vintage, 1995.

88. "When Leather is a Whip" by Martín Espada. From *Alabanza: New and Selected Poems 1982-2002*. New York, NY: W.W. Norton & Company, 2004.

89. "Late Fragment" by Raymond Carver. From *A New Path to the Waterfall*. Boston, MA: Atlantic Monthly Press, 1989.

90. https://bukowski.net/poems/back_to_the_machine_gun.php

91. Quote about Charles Bukowski from Michael Greenberg in the *Boston Review* http://bostonreview.net/archives/BR19.3/fiction.html

92. Saunders, George. "My Writing Education: A Timeline." *The New Yorker*, October 22, 2015. https://www.newyorker.com/books/page-turner/my-writing-education-a-timeline Date accessed September 2, 2019.

93. McIntosh, Emma, and Alex McKeen. "Overrepresentation of Indigenous people in Canada's prisons persists amid drop in overall incarceration." *The Star*. June 19, 2018. https://www.thestar.com/news/canada/2018/06/19/overrepresentation-of-indigenous-people-in-canadas-prisons-persists-amid-drop-in-overall-incarceration.html Date accessed August 3, 2019.

94. "On Attachement" by Suzanne Buffam. From *The Irrationalist*. Toronto, ON: House of Anansi Press, 2010.

95. "Alone" by Maya Angelou. https://poets.org/poem/alone

96. Cole, Teju. *Open City*. New York, NY: Random House, 2011.

97. "Oranges" by Gary Soto. https://www.poetryfoundation.org/poetrymagazine/browse?contentId=35513

98. "ICU" by Spencer Reece. From *The Road to Emmaus*. New York, NY: Farrar, Straus and Giroux, 2015.

99. Chung, Sonya. "Post-40 Bloomer: Spencer Reece, The Poet's Tale." *MM The Millions*. May 2, 2012. https://themillions.com/2012/05/post-40-bloomer-spencer-reece-the-poets-tale.html

100. "The Kindness of the Blind" by Wislawa Szymborska. August 1, 2004. https://www.newyorker.com/magazine/2004/08/09/the-kindness-of-the-blind

101. "You Learn" by Jorge Luis Borges. hellopoetry.com/poem/670010/you-learn-by-jorge-luis-borges

102. Shelley, Mary. *Frankenstein*. Ed. Johanna M. Smith Boston, MA: Bedford Books, 1992. Page 90. The film *Mary Shelley's Frankenstein* was directed by Kevin Branagh and released by Tristar Pictures in 1994.

103 Rao, Sameer. "Kendrick Lamar's Reaction to Police Brutality: 'Rage Is The Perfect Word For It'" Colorlines. December 15, 2015. https://www.colorlines.com/articles/kenrick-lamars-reacation-police-brutality-rage-perfect-word-it Date accessed August 5, 2019.